The U.S. Economy Demystified

The Meaning of U.S. Business Statistics and What They Portend for the Future

Third Edition

Albert T. Sommers

with
Lucie R. Blau

LEXINGTON BOOKS
An Imprint of Macmillan, Inc.
New York

Maxwell Macmillan Canada
Toronto

Maxwell Macmillan International
New York   Oxford   Singapore   Sydney

Library of Congress Cataloging-in-Publication Data

Sommers, Albert T.
    The U.S. economy demystified : the meaning of U.S. business
statistics and what they portend for the future / Albert T.
Sommers, with Lucie R. Blau. —3rd ed.
        p.   cm.
    ISBN 0–02–930115–7 (cloth) — ISBN 0–02–930116–5 (paper)
    1. United States—Economic conditions—1945– 2. United States—
Economic policy. 3. National income—United States—Accounting.
I. Blau, Lucie R. II. Title. III. Title: United States economy
demystified.
HC106.5.S64   1993
330.973'0928—dc20   92–34701
                                                     CIP

Lexington Books
An Imprint of Macmillan, Inc.
866 Third Avenue, New York, N. Y. 10022

Maxwell Macmillan Canada, Inc.
1200 Eglinton Avenue East
Suite 200
Don Mills, Ontario M3C 3N1

Macmillan, Inc. is part of the Maxwell Communication
Group of Companies.

Printed in the United States of America

printing number
1   2   3   4   5   6   7   8   9   10

Contents

Figures and Tables

Figures

Tables

Foreword

This book developed out of the author's experience over four decades in explaining the workings of the U.S. economic system and the significance of economic statistics to the thousands of business executives and government officials, here and abroad, who constitute The Conference Board audience. The statistical materials with which it deals, and the economic and philosophical questions to which it addresses itself, are drawn out of long exposure to the interests expressed by intelligent laypersons on how this immensely fascinating economic system works and how the evidence of its workings can be observed. Mr. Sommers writes as he speaks—lucidly, and with ingratiating humility regarding the uncertainties of data and the limits of economic reasoning.

Lucie R. Blau, the author's long-time research associate, worked prodigiously on the underlying statistics, contributed to the design of the figures and tables, and supervised the preparation of the text for publication. Chuck N. Tow, The Conference Board's chief chartist, was in charge of the graphics. Elizabeth Ahlin managed the text through its several drafts. The book is really a joint product of all these people.

Preston Townley
President and CEO
The Conference Board

Preface to the Third Edition

S ince the first edition of this book went to press seven years ago, the U.S. economy has behaved in mysterious ways that have confounded the efforts of governmental and private economists to forecast its near-term course or even to understand its behavior in the recent past. Particularly in the years since 1987, domestic economic conditions have turned seriously sluggish and, on the whole, unsatisfactory in the face of massive stimuli provided by economic policy itself, as well as by such presumably favorable accidents as an enormous reduction in the price of crude oil and petroleum products, and a striking recovery in the demand for exports. This apparent paradox—the unseemly reluctance of the system to enjoy circumstances that virtually all forecasters considered highly favorable—does not reflect defects in the statistical system itself, and the chapters of this book concerned primarily with such matters have required very little revision. But other chapters that deal more substantively with the behavior of the system—particularly, the behavior of the financial side of the system—have required some rewriting and, here and there, considerable amplification. Finally, pursuit of an explanation of the paradox has called for additional material on the historical development of the United States over several decades, and the bearing of that history on its recent and prospective economic behavior has required the addition of an entire chapter on the longer-term outlook.

In these new materials and in the additions and revisions of later chapters in the book, a sense of urgency appears—an impression that large and unfamiliar issues confront the U.S. economy and, therefore, its business leaders, its government policy makers, and inevitably its citizens, both as producers and as consumers. Dealing with emerging and still evolving issues in which evidence and perception can change rapidly is awkward material for a book, with its inevitably lengthy production schedule. This poses a risk for reader and writer alike—the risk of high perishability. But there is no way of avoiding the risk at this critical juncture in the course of the U.S. economy.

The authors are greatly indebted to the large number of readers of earlier editions, whose comments and suggestions have improved this edition's accuracy and readability. For any remaining errors, each author blames the other.

Introduction

Immensely powerful, ever changing, pulsating with a hundred different rhythms, and offering every conceivable combination of economic risk and reward, the U.S. economy ranks as one of the wonders of the world. As a subject for detached intellectual study, it offers fascinations and degrees of complexity unsurpassed by any structures in the physical world.

But it is, of course, more than that: It is the natural habitat in which we live, work, save, spend, plan, invest. Each of us can expect to grow familiar with, and then finally expert in, the area of this structure in which we make our own careers, but each area is inseparably bound to the whole, and often takes its course from conditions and trends arising in distant parts of the system. The prosperity of families, businesses, and even governmental units in the structure depends not only on sophisticated adjustment to the local environment, but also on a reasonable grasp of the course of the whole system. That, in turn, requires some facility in reading and interpreting the awesome profusion of signals thrown off by the economic system as it makes its way through time. The collection and processing of these signals is an industry in itself, largely but not exclusively in the hands of government agencies.

If the U.S. economy is a wonder to behold, this book is about how to behold it. It is not for professional economists, who spend their lives creating, handling, and interpreting the kinds of information offered here. Instead, it is for the sophisticated businessperson, the financial executive, the private investor, even the alert individual consumer, who seek a compact, digestible guide to the general evidence on economic conditions and require a framework within which to insert new information as it appears in the media—who want to apply their own practical intelligence to the question of where the U.S. economy is, judging from its statistical condition, and where it is likely to go. It will not make the reader his or her own economist (there are those who say there are too many around already); but a reasonably careful study should considerably improve his or her ability to understand the evidence, to keep track of it, to develop confidence in his or her knowledge of current economic events, and to sense the probable range of future developments.

The first chapter of this book puts the present position of the U.S. economy in a long historical perspective that is essential to understanding its present behavior and the issues it will confront in the remainder of this decade. The next two chapters lay out the essentials of the U.S. statistical system, starting with the national accounting system, without which no understanding of the position and course of the economy is really possible, and moving on to brief descriptions of the basic array of statistics that describe U.S. economic performance. Chapter 4 explains the nature of the business cycle and the statistics by which this powerful tidal current in the system can be observed and measured and, at times, predicted. Chapter 5 deals with the influences exerted on the course of the system by the conscious decisions of government with respect to the course of the federal budget, the availability and price of credit, and the general (recently spectacular) behavior of the financial markets. Chapter 6 places the U.S. economy in its world context; it treats briefly those statistical relationships that describe our place in the world economy and the consequences that flow from our international behavior. Chapter 7 interprets the evidence on U.S. performance with respect to inflation—the enemy that awaits the system when it loses its coherence or when it seeks excessively costly goals. Chapter 8 appraises the outlook for the United States in the decade of the Nineties. In particular, it analyzes the immense strains exerted on the system by the excesses of the 1980s, and their serious consequences for the future growth rate of the system as a whole.

Much of standard economics treats economic life as transpiring in a so-called free market, in which individual self-interest reigns supreme. This is not the way the real world works, of course; some of the greatest difficulties in understanding the behavior of the economy reflect this disparity between theory and reality. Accordingly, a final chapter, more reflective and less numerical, continues an appraisal, begun in chapter 8, of the U.S. economy as a component of a total sociological structure subject to social, political, and ethical pressures that often influence its course and limit its options.

1

The Long Wave of History

A
ny effort to comprehend and then to explain an economic system must begin, not with theory and not with statistics, but with history. At all times and for all nations, economic systems are the products of an evolutionary process; they carry their history with them—if not visibly on their surfaces, then deep inside, in mechanisms and structures that affect their course in the future. The events of the past few weeks, or even the past few years, color and shape the present and shed light on where the system will go next. But even far more distant events—rhythms born even decades ago— may still be pulsing in the system, influencing its behavior in ways that are unpredictable from the evidence at the surface. Great wars, great depressions, great booms are not passing events whose significance disappears as the events themselves come to an end; they are capable of reorganizing and redirecting economic systems, throwing them into new trajectories that can run for decades, producing economic experience that cannot be understood without reference to them.

If this is true of all economies at all times, it is spectacularly true of the postwar U.S. economy. The record of its particular past, traceable to great events half a century ago, is controlling much of its behavior, producing results— in the real economy, and in the behavior of its financial sector— that are inexplicable without reference to its history. Here, in these understudied and partly forgotten roots of the future, is where we must begin.

Any observer of the American economic scene over several decades would almost certainly agree with the observation that life in the U.S. economy is now more complex, more difficult to understand, and more hazardous to predict than it used to be. In particular, the two conventional modalities of economic forecasting—the eighteen-month, short-term forecast, and the ten-year, long-term projection—carry much less conviction than they seemed to hold for businesspersons and policymakers even a decade ago. The tools of short-term economic analysis have shed little light on the outlook. The typical short-term forecast running quarterly for eighteen months or so into the future has been unrewarding—which is to say it has frequently failed to identify the business-cycle phase of the system and almost always missed the speed of cyclical recovery. It is commonly observed that the business cycle, on which short-term forecasting depended, has partly atrophied. (Not so; see chapter 4.)

The decade-long projections also seem to have fallen into disuse. To project ten years out takes a long base of past data, on a kind of cantilever principle; but it is hard to find long economic series that seem to retain relevance for the radically different domestic and international circumstances in which the United States has found itself in the early 1990s. Long-term projections, drawn out of long-term calculations of past trends, almost necessarily take a linear form. The turbulent, volatile history of the U.S. economy over the past decade hardly seems to be effectively expressed by linear projection.

In the past fifteen years, economics has thus seemed to provide little real guidance, either to economic policy or to the management of real and financial assets. This is not a matter of inadequate information or failures of economic reasoning; the data and intellectual resources available to economists, as they are reviewed in later chapters of this book, are impressive, and they worked well for decades. But more than ever before, they seem to require a coherent, historically based view of how the system got here and, therefore, a view of the social and political, as well as economic, forces carrying it into the future. A description of the current U.S. economic position as reflecting history, even a "long wave" of history—a complex, nonlinear trajectory, incorporating in its later phases the fortunes of many of our trading partners—seems to offer a perspective essential to our purposes here. It seems to clarify the present and illuminate the main issues of the future, as described in chapter 8. It heightens the sense of danger that is now felt, and more and more expressed, by economists and financial analysts; but it also provides some essential understanding of what the dangers are, and what requirements they impose on us if they are to be averted.

Historical Origins; the Big Bang

Where to start such a history? For once, economics provides an unequivocal answer. Conditions prevailing at the end of World War II—almost half a century ago—qualify spectacularly as a time of gross discordance in world economic conditions, containing a huge (without question, the biggest in history) volume of static economic energy available to the United States—an unprecedented voltage accumulated over ten years of worldwide depression, and then five years of very nearly total war. This massive disruption of the normal course of history—the gross and prolonged deferrals of the ordinary satisfactions of life—marks the beginning of modern history.

In the years of the Great Depression, the American economic system was reshaped and its history restarted. The structure of private debt was collapsed by bankruptcy, repossession, and default in an environment that tolerated little or no new debt incurrence (see figure 1–1). At the same time, levels of holdings of real assets shriveled in the virtual absence of new production. The shrunken stock of physical assets that survived the depression was old in years and old relative to the technology available at the end of the depression (technological development, but not commercialization of the findings, continued at a rapid rate, even under depression conditions). At the end of the Thirties, the U.S. system was depleted, even near exhaustion, in all its physical dimensions; it carried large deficits in the physical stock of goods required to maintain predepression living standards (see figure 1–2).

The ensuing five years of total war continued to suppress the level of real nondefense assets, whose average technological age continued to lengthen. But whole new ranges of technology, developed initially for military purposes but holding vast promise for commercial exploitation, accumulated during the war. The war also produced another crucial requirement for explosive growth that only war is likely to generate: an enormous increase in liquidity, reflecting the gigantic financial requirements of a wartime government and the absolute necessity for the central bank to provide the financing. The financing of the war produced a "Keynesian shock" of liquid-

Figure 1–1. Fifteen Years of Low Debt Formation

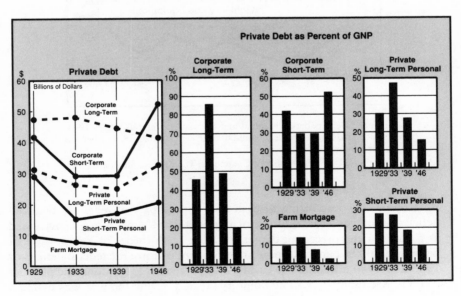

Sources: U.S. Department of Commerce; The Conference Board.

Figure 1–2. Fifteen Years of Shortfalls in Demand

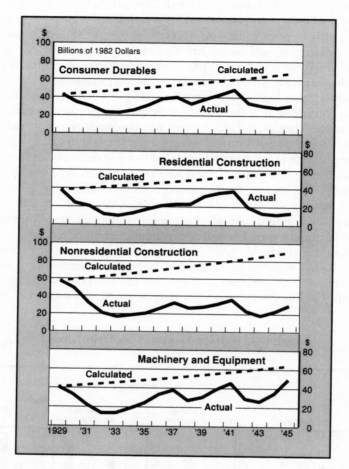

Notes: Deficits between actual and calculated demands, 1929–1945; calculated series represent cumulative growth from 1929, at 3 percent per annum.

Sources: U.S. Department of Commerce; The Conference Board.

ity growth—an outpouring of cash as a counterpart of federally financed deficits—that was a vast multiple of anything that Keynes himself envisioned as a cure for the preceding depression. The birth throes of a new wave of history should be expected to be of heroic proportions; the federal deficits of 1943 and 1944 amounted to twenty-five percent of gross domestic product (*GDP*)! (See figure 1–3.) The liquidity created during the war was deflated in only small degree by rising prices, since prices (and wages) were subjected to the most effective government control in all of history.

Figure 1–3. The Federal Budget in Depression and War

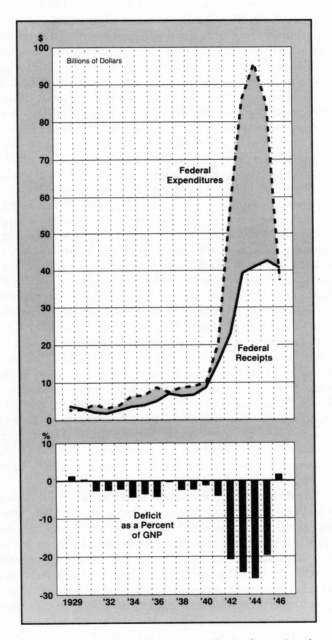

Sources: U.S. Department of Commerce; The Conference Board.

To these necessary domestic conditions for a "big bang" and a restarting of economic history should be added the fact that the United States emerged from World War II in a condition of international economic and technological dominance unsurpassed in the history of any nation. Its most effective industrial competitors, Japan and Germany, had suffered industrial ruin; the allies of the United States also suffered varying degrees of damage, while U.S. territory and its industrial facilities were untouched. The United States emerged into the postwar world in a near vacuum of international competition, equipped with the world's only industrial base. Its currency—the only reserve currency— commanded such immense respect that for twenty-five years it was preferred to the gold for which it was freely exchangeable at $35 an ounce. Indeed, the most serious international problem confronting the developed world after World War II was the threat that a "dollar shortage" would inhibit the growth of international trade. The International Monetary Fund's "special drawing rights," the SDRs, were invented to add to the world's liquidity at a time when foreign supplies of the dollar simply could not increase (that is, the United States could not run a deficit requiring settlement in dollars). The United States ran a trade surplus in every postwar year until 1971; its first significant deficit on current account was in 1977; its net investment income reached a peak in 1981.

A final ingredient in the initial energy of this wave of history was a unique intersection of attitudinal and cultural trends. The trauma of the Great Depression had produced a violent liberalization of the legislative structure of the economy, seeking to provide assurance—in many respects literally *insurance*—that the experience of the 1930s would never recur. The philosophical substructure of this change was ratified early in the postwar years by the Employment Act of 1946, which imposed responsibility for prosperity on the government itself and validated the creation of such antirecession, prosecurity institutions (many of them created in skeleton form in the 1930s) as social security, unemployment compensation, bank deposit guarantees, and farm debt and mortgage guarantees. (It took forty years for some of these *insurance* policies to ripen into the formidable liabilities they impose on government today.)

But while the depression liberalized the structure of the system, it had a powerfully conservative impact on the behavior of people as consumers and businesspersons. This conservative, risk-averse set of attitudes survived far into the postwar years, deferring and modulating the inevitable liquidation of the imposed increase in security through increased risk assumption. It is a valid principle of economics (valid, even if hard to demonstrate statistically) that nonmarket increments to security produced by a socioeconomic system (social security, unemployment insurance, deposit insurance, health insurance, and so forth) will in time be liquidated by lower saving and higher debt incurrence (as they were with a vengeance in the 1980s; see chapter 8). The inflationary implications of the immense increase in liquidity attributable to war financing, and the inflationary implications of the great social programs installed during the Thirties, lay dormant for almost three decades, as attitudes toward debt and risk remained strikingly conservative. (For ten years after the war ended, the average term on automobile installment credit stayed below two years.)

To conclude on this spectacular experience, there has never been a more violent rupture of conventional economic relationships than in the fifteen years of U.S. history ending with peace in 1945. The end of World War II marked an explosive release of energy and a spectacular new dawn for the U.S. economy. The multiple generation of World War II veterans, fifteen million strong, that poured into the U.S. labor market in 1945 and 1946 started their careers in the morning light of a great boom.

The Wave in Descent

Mornings do not last forever, and booms consume their energies as they go. Granting the awesome original energy involved, historical tracing of the course of the postwar explosion through time should nevertheless not be expected to be easy, or to reveal a high degree of regularity, periodicity, or a clear continuity of evidence; the underlying history is a complex aggregate of many interweaving forces. It is subject to modifications attributable to the stops and starts of the short-term business cycle, alterations of short-term economic policy, variations in the behavior of other economies with which the United States has trade and financial relationships, and floodtides and then abatements in major domestic markets (for example, the suburbanization nexus of demands for housing, roads, automobiles, and then schools arising out of the postwar elevation of the birthrate—all of them now in decline).

Developments in all these more local conditions are described in later chapters. But what appears in the aggregate history is progressive exhaustion of the strengths out of which the wave originated; progressive deteriorations in liquidity and in the debt burden; gradual engagement of, and then increased dependence on, the public insurance programs legislated in the depression and progressively expanded in the first three postwar decades; increasingly reluctant response of the system to the conventional stimuli provided by economic policy; and reversal of the huge resources of economic energy available in the international dominance of the United States in 1945. In the 1980s, the energy of the "big bang" was exhausted in a final explosion; since then, economic experience has changed strikingly. It is now halting and uncertain, as though seeking a new ground zero from which to begin again a cycle of growth.

The private debt burden would now appear to be mature by almost any criterion. In the late 1980s, ratios of debt to the income flows that must service them were high throughout the private sector (see figure 1–4). Defaults and bankruptcies rose sharply in the housing market and in installment credit. A violent burst of default prevailed in the agricultural economy for several earlier years; in the late 1980s and early 1991, massive defaults in junk bonds occurred. In the automobile market and in the housing market, the terms of loans had stopped rising several years ago; in earlier stages of the wave, rejuvenation of debt formation was periodically achieved by further lengthening of average terms.

Characteristically for a period of weak underlying general business conditions, the federal deficit, which had grown substantially throughout the 1980s, soared again. The accumulating federal debt has recently exploded at a rate far greater than the growth of aggregate debt, so that the share of federal debt in the total is rising, as it characteristically does during such periods. The ratio of the federal debt to a year's GDP was about 1.0 at the end of war financing in 1946; it fell almost without interruption in the course of the postwar boom, reaching a trough of about 0.33 in 1981; it has since risen to about 0.67.

The debt burden in the late 1980s was made more onerous by a subdued rate of inflation. Inflation itself was constrained throughout the earlier stages of the wave; it accelerated during the 1970s, and began subsiding late in that decade and in the 1980s, mainly for reasons involving currency values, trends in international trade, and the collapse of oil prices. Whatever else may be said of it, inflation is at least an indication of strong underlying demand, and of the dominance of sellers (of labor as well as of goods) over buyers. In the slowing of the late 1980s, the absence of inflation left debt still rising, without benefit of inflationary expansions of income. In other words, continuing growth of the debt in the late 1980s was no longer sufficiently stimulative to maintain comparable growth in incomes. For much of the last half of the 1980s, the growth rate of both public and private debt was double the growth rate of nominal GDP, and four times the inflation of prices and incomes.

Earlier in the decade, the agricultural sector stood as a gross illustration of the interweaving of the waves of debt and inflation and of the final position in which debt moves from stimulus to burden. In the late 1980s, debt became a powerful restraint on most parts of the system, causing gross deterioration in the markets for housing and consumer durables.

During much of the 1980s, again, the velocity of money (the speed at which money turns over) fell in the real world of output and income, but it increased enormously in financial markets, which experienced a vast multiplication of secondary security volume (mortgage-backed securities, packaged receivables, mutual fund issuance, and so forth), and an accompanying explosion in volume. Thus, the enormous pyramiding of credits in the late 1980s seems, in part, to have bypassed the real world and to have been absorbed in financial turnover. The high real interest rates that seem to prevail

Figure 1–4. The Maturing of the Debt Burden

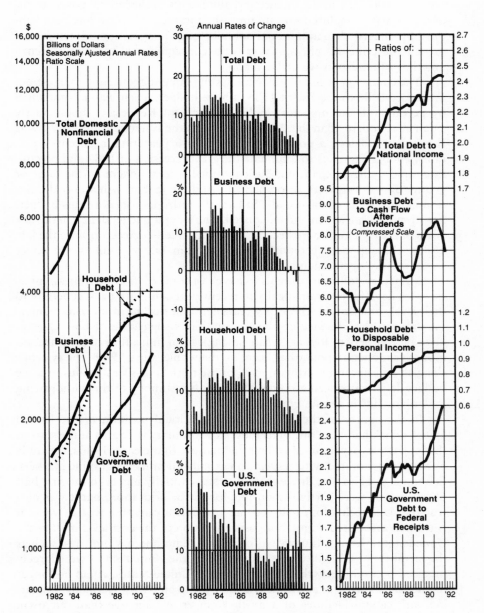

Sources: Federal Reserve; U.S. Department of Commerce; The Conference Board.

in the U.S. economy even today reflect this ravenous appetite of the financial sector, particularly in the financing requirements of the federal government, at a time when the inflation rate prevailing in the real world has been subdued by sluggish demand. It does not take much imagination or picturesque prose to describe this phenomenon as the consequence of speculative frenzy at a time of unresponsive real demand.

The condition of fiscal policy carries the same suggestion of exhaustion. From late 1982 to the end of 1986, a huge budget deficit was accompanied by accommodative monetary policy—a kind of Keynesian shock, vastly smaller, of course, than the shock delivered to the system during World War II but, nevertheless, a powerful stimulus for a peacetime economy— certainly enough stimulus to terminate the great recession of 1982 and precipitate rapid cyclical expansion. But continued federal deficits of the same or greater dimensions were accompanied by falling real growth and real inflation in later years of the decade. In fact, the reflection of enormous budgetary stimulus is now dim and exhausted. The federal budget deficit in the last years of the postwar boom became less and less self-correcting; since the late 1980s, the supposed economic stimulus from budget deficits no longer seems to have operated at all.

Monetary policy, too, seems to have lost some of its effectiveness. Interest rates have fallen dramatically in recent years, and are back generally to their levels of ten and even twenty years ago. The decline in short-term interest rates, in the presence of several conditions suggestive of high rates (a huge budget deficit, low aggregate saving), is an indication of how accommodative monetary policy has been, on the whole, since 1989. The system's sluggish and uncertain growth, in response to the massive stimulus of large budget deficits financed accommodatively, is testimony to the withdrawing underlying tide in the system.

In the course of the 1980s, the international position of the United States, which had been one of its most extraordinary strengths at the start of the long wave, experienced violent fluctuation. In the early 1980s, the trade position deteriorated with respect to virtually all of its geographic markets. Economic policies that drove the dollar substantially higher in the first half of the decade were partly responsible for the deterioration, but it was also true that U.S. technology had become available around the world, where it was often associated with labor costs a fraction of the cost level built in the United States through thirty years of an ascendant boom. Countries (such as the members of OPEC), whose imports from the United States were largely financed by rapid growth of loans from the United States, could no longer finance the loans. Our erstwhile enemies, Japan and West Germany, operating with capital facilities of a much younger average age than our own, began to run in the one instance a large, and in the other instance a gigantic, trade surplus with the United States. In the course of the deficits of the early 1980s, the United States became a net borrower in international financial markets, to such a degree that the entire surplus of investment abroad over foreign investment in the United States was wiped out by 1985 (see figure 1–5). At the end of 1986, the net debt to foreigners exceeded $250 billion, and it continued to grow in ensuing years, reaching $600 billion by 1990.

In the late years of the decade and continuing into the 1990s, a fall in the dollar as dramatic as its rise in the first half of the decade produced a pronounced decline in the trade deficit, and the entire current-account position in the United States has recently improved substantially. Nevertheless, in the world of the 1990s, the United States faces powerful technical competence and export potentials on the part of some of the very countries that desperately required U.S. financial assistance at the end of the world war.

These changes—in debt position, in liquidity, in inflation, in response to policy stimulus, in international trade position—can be viewed as individual deteriorations in individual areas. But their interconnections are substantial; taken together, viewed as interactive and living history, they describe progressive involution of virtually all the conditions on which the birth of America's unparalleled postwar prosperity rested. Ever since 1988, the real growth of the U.S. economy has been slowing. In the Summer of 1990, after a final and unsustainable burst of growth in debt and at the onset of the Gulf War, the system collapsed into cyclical recession that lasted, with a minor interruption, to the end of 1991. The recession, occurring in the presence of all that policy stimulus, may properly be taken to mark the end of the long wave of economic history described here. In fact, the culmination of the boom and its inevitable reversal is now at least a few years in the past; the system is now already well into a struggle to offset a cumulative drain on its energies and to establish a firm new basis for ongoing growth— all these issues being the subject of chapter 8.

Worldview

For nearly a century, the United States has been the indisputable world leader in terms of the size of its domestic markets. In the years after World War II, it was also the world's largest source of capital. The Marshall Plan, and then the awesome wave of U.S. investment in manufacturing facilities in Europe and North America, as well as in energy in the Middle East, and then finally its credit extension to less-developed countries (the LDCs), distributed its assets and influence to almost all parts of the world. It was, truly, the world's locomotive. The United States now shares dominance with a recovered Europe and the surging economies of the Pacific Rim—itself evidence of its changed position in history. But the sheer size of its markets retains for it a crucial position in the world economy.

By the middle of 1986, it was becoming clear that a time of troubles in the United States was beginning to have an impact on other developed econ-

Figure 1–5. The Decline in the U.S. International Investment Position

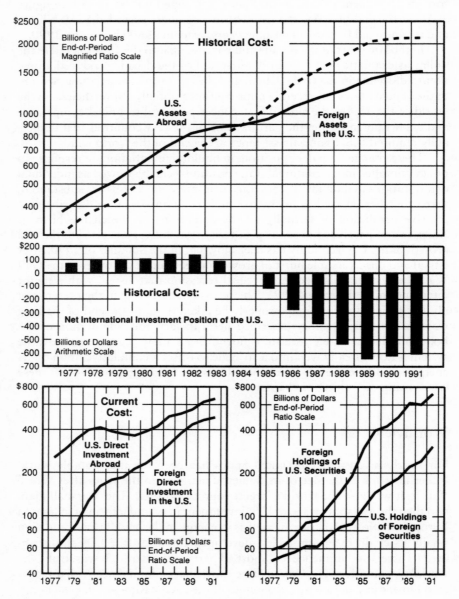

Sources: U.S. Department of Commerce; The Conference Board.

omies, at least partly through the consequences of the devaluation of the dollar, but also partly because the downdrift in U.S. economic energy was reducing the role of the world's largest economy as a locomotive. As the effects of the declining dollar have become more visible in Europe and Japan, concern over the sluggish, apparently compromised growth rate of the United States has broadened into a concern that the whole *developed* world (therefore, the *whole* world) is in a phase of dwindling economic energy, failing growth rates, and, conceivably, serious international recession. The ultimate exhaustion of the long wave in the United States has thus spread to the developed world as a whole.

The deteriorated long-term performance of the U.S. economy was bound, in time, to affect all the other developed economies with which the United States trades heavily. This is true, even though the relative success of those other economies (principally, of course, West Germany and Japan), is a major reason that U.S. experience deteriorated. This circularity is typical of economic process: The weakened U.S. market and its weakened currency (in a longer-term perspective) are now arresting the growth of those economies that prospered by exporting to it.

With respect to trade, there is no longer an energized voltage gap within the universe of the developed economies. Instead, the energy lies between that universe and the universe of newly industrialized countries (the NICs) equipped with advanced technology but still experiencing far lower costs and living standards. The NICs—South Korea, Taiwan, Hong Kong, Malaysia, Brazil, Mexico, and now China— constitute a new economic presence out there, an unprecedented combination of high technology and low cost. They are young, vigorous, hungry, unencumbered by high living standards. They grew up largely unobserved in the shadow of the American boom. The evidence of their broad and pervasive invasion into the world of the developed economies is growing more evident all the time. In the presence of rapid growth among developing economies, trade outcomes among the developed economies no longer constitute a zero-sum game.

The United States is thus no longer a net contributor of energy to the developed world. The long wave, so clearly traceable to the explosion of 1946, and so readily documented through the four-decade trajectory reviewed here, might now be said to have been internationalized, as the United States struggles to support its growth rate, as well as to support a living standard developed in the soaring years of the first postwar quarter-century. The unresponsiveness of the U.S. economy to economic policy stimulus and the extreme rate of growth of foreign debt on the part of the United States are evidence that a locomotive role for the United States is no longer possible.

If the generally prosperous condition of the developed world in the years of this history was born in the enlightened exercise of unprecedented dominance by the American economy starting at the end of World War II, then no comparable rebirth seems to be visible on the horizon. This by no means argues that the United States, or the rest of the developed world, faces an unavoidable encounter with deep and prolonged recession. But it does suggest that there are only modest policy opportunities for supporting, and then gradually rebuilding, a universe that has consumed its inherited energies and is struggling to maintain modest growth. The U.S. economy must now live in the present. The lesson of this history is not panic but prudent caution, exercised at least until the new world we have entered reveals more clearly its promises and dangers. The history also suggests that standard reasoning of the past that worked in a period of American supremacy will require constant and careful appraisal to ensure that it still works in a world so greatly altered by the end of an era.

If there is an ultimate caution in this history, it lies in the seeming unwillingness of the United States to recognize its new position and to act accordingly. The United States cannot hope to return to more vigorous growth until it comes to grips with the passionate dedication to consumption it developed during its decades of world supremacy. Probably the most important contribution the United States can make to its own future and, therefore, to the future of the world economy would be an elevation of its real saving rate—to provide for its own capital requirements by constraining its consumption, thereby freeing resources for export and for investment at home. The later chapters of this book, dealing with issues of the business cycle, of inflation, of government policies, and of the world environment, make, over and over again, the point of the need for a new national governance in U.S. economic behavior, one that recognizes the social as well as economic realities of the U.S. economic situation in the 1990s. These issues are appraised at length in chapter 8.

2

The National Economic Accounting System

The U.S. national accounting system—previously referred to as the GNP accounts and now as the GDP accounts—is a magnificent summary of economic activity in the United States, packed with information for business executives and their advisers. The accounts represent the apex of an immense statistical pyramid provided by public and private agencies engaged in the collection of economic and business statistics. The accounting structure of the national accounts organizes this enormous flow of data under consistent accounting definitions and concepts, and builds them into a coherent portrait of aggregate economic activity. The accounts are available quarterly. Their earliest release, normally about twenty-five days after the end of a quarter, is a very big statistical event, celebrated and analyzed throughout the business world. Two progressive revisions, incorporating more and more detailed knowledge of events, appear in the ensuing two months; the month after that produces the first preliminary estimate for the next quarter. Life among the statistics has thus been so arranged that there is a GDP released every month—a great convenience for the writers of monthly economic letters.

The preliminary release and the later revisions are the best and most complete general portrait of what is happening in all the major sectors of the U.S. economy. Additionally, they provide a great statistical skeleton of the history described above, all the way back to 1929. The U.S. national accounts are widely considered to be the best and most promptly available economic accounts in the world.

In today's world, in which broad trends in economic activity and policy decisions have prompt and powerful implications for individual markets, a reasonable working knowledge of this accounting system would seem to be as important to the business executive as is a working knowledge of business accounting. The national accounts serve the same general purpose—namely, to provide the stockholders (that's us) with a summary overview of the condition and direction of the U.S. economy viewed as a giant, departmentalized business generating streams of output and streams of income.

The aggregate summary character of the national accounts has also inevitably made them the principal vehicle of aggregate economic forecasting; the accounts are, in fact, the very language in which general forecasts are couched. Making efficient use of the economic forecasts available, relating them to activities of an individual firm, and drawing from them the prospects for policy variables, such as interest rates and taxes, requires a basic understanding of the national accounting system.

This summary description of the national accounts is intended to serve just these purposes—to provide a framework for grasping the significance of each new quarterly set as it makes its appearance in the press and to provide a basis for comparing actual developments in the economy with those projected by the forecasting fraternity.

In addition to their utility in appraising current and prospective economic conditions, the national accounts represent the statistical universe to which economic policy is applied. Budget estimates of the federal government rest on assumptions with respect to the course of the national economy, as described in the national accounts. Monetary policy draws its objectives from the condition of the system and the relative desirability of stimulus or constraint in the light of present behavior, as revealed in the quarterly release of the national accounts. Thus, sensing the probable course of these important influences on economic activity (and particularly on financial markets) also depends on a knowledge of the national accounts.

For all their jargon and the occasional exotic departures from familiar accounting that are required for so complex an economic system, the national accounts stand as the jewel of U.S. statistics. It is difficult to convey the richness of detail available in the total set of accounts; the reader is urged to refer to the annual national-accounts issue of the *Survey of Current Business,* appearing every July (published by the U.S. Department of Commerce), which revises and updates the entire system, always carrying the revision back several years on the basis of newly available data.

The Structure of the Accounts

The conceptual structure of the national accounts bears a powerful family resemblance to ordinary accounting. It has its own peculiarities, and its nomenclature is necessarily somewhat special. The accounting principles themselves, however, are on the whole simple, logical, and reasonably familiar; there are peculiarities, but no mysteries. Even the peculiarities are rational responses to the special problems posed by accounting for all the activities of a vast, diversified entity that incorporates governmental as well as private activity and (unlike a private corporation) consumes virtually all of its own output.

The U.S. economy described in these accounts can be thought of as a giant company, employing the whole working population, producing all consumer goods (which it sells in its company store) and all the capital goods it requires for its own production facilities, while providing its employees with incomes and benefits, and borrowing back their savings to invest for the future. To keep a running record of all these activities, the conceptual structure incorporates the following basic principles.

Double-Entry Bookkeeping

The national accounts are a double-entry bookkeeping system, recording the total economic output of the economy on the one hand and tabulating all the resulting income flows on the other hand.

The total income flows generated by the system—the compensation of employees, the earnings of the self-employed, the earnings from real and financial property—are conceptually equal to the value of the total output (with a few minor qualifications discussed later). Think of a typical business operating statement: If the net income before taxes is thought of as payment to capital, then total costs (including depreciation) equal total gross revenues (see figure 2–1).

Avoiding Double Counting of Output

The output side of the account is generally restricted to counting the output of finished product.

It would obviously grossly overstate output if the production and sale of intermediate products were included in the total. For example, if we count the steel (produced by a steel company) and *then* count the automobiles (produced by an automobile producer) that incorporate the steel, we would be counting the steel twice. The value of the steel is embedded in the value of the car.

The method of adding is equivalent to summing up the *value added* at each level of production—that is, the wage costs, capital costs (including profit), and depreciation costs experienced by the seller and embedded in the selling price. For each seller, it is the equivalent of sales, less costs on purchases from others. Intermediate purchases thus wash out of the total. The one exception to this count is in the treatment of inventory. Production of steel that appears as an *increase* in steel inventories, held by producers and consumers of steel, must be counted as output; here, double counting is avoided, since the steel has not yet been sold in a final product. Increases in *all* inventory (including such finished products as automobiles in dealer stocks) are included in the sum of output.

Figure 2–1. Output Equals Income

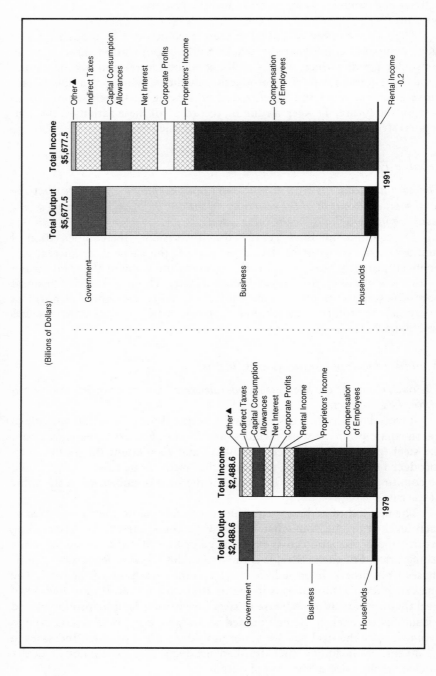

(Billions of Dollars)

▲Includes statistical discrepancy.

Sources: U.S. Department of Commerce; The Conference Board.

Output is Valued at Market

The accounts value the physical outputs at market prices— that is, at their sales price.

A special condition arises here, because not all output actually passes through a market. An easy illustration is food produced on a farm but consumed by the farm family. In this instance, the accounts estimate the market value and add it to the *output* (and to the *income,* and to the *expenditures*) of farm households. Such estimates are called *imputed income* and *imputed expenditure.* Other, more complicated forms of this problem appear in the housing industry (discussed later in this chapter). Government output (mostly services performed by government employees) is generally valued at its cost to the government, but the great bulk of output is valued at a market price (see figure 2–2).

From GNP to GDP

Until 1991, the aggregate total of activity was known affectionately as the **GNP:** In that form, the measure included income flows (dividends and interest) generated by American investment in the rest of the world (for example, the dividends and interest earned offshore by subsidiaries of U.S. companies). And it excluded dividends and interest earned in the United States by subsidiaries of foreign-owned companies. The GNP total was thus based on ownership of assets.

In 1991, the U.S. Department of Commerce altered the accounts to include all income and dividends earned in the United States regardless of who owned them; and to exclude such income earned outside the United States by U.S. corporations. The resulting series, called *gross domestic product,* is thus now a *geographically defined* total, rather than a *property-defined* (or "command basis") total.

Since the United States earned more abroad than other countries earned in the United States, the GDP is less than the GNP, by about thirteen billion dollars in 1991. All of the difference appears in the "net exports" component of the GDP (see below).

The GDP is Gross

The total output of the system is usually referred to simply as GDP—**gross domestic product.** The term *gross* is required because the aggregate does not make a deduction for the exhaustion of capital in producing the output— *that is, it is before a depreciation deduction.* (In national accounting, depreciation is referred to as **consumption of fixed capital.**) In addition to ordinary business assets, the accounts also treat residential properties as depreciable assets.

Figure 2–2. Value of Output

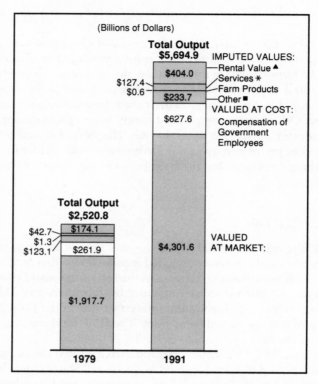

▲Includes farm and nonfarm housing, rental values of nonprofit institutions.
★By financial intermediaries, except life insurance carriers.
■Includes employee-related food, clothing, and shelter; and miscellaneous housing and equipment.
Sources: U.S. Department of Commerce; The Conference Board.

Capital Gains and Losses Excluded

It should be borne in mind that the national accounts are a purified set of statistics—*purified to remove the creation or destruction of values that have nothing to do with actual output or income earned in the accounting period.* A rise in the price level would elevate the value of a constant stock of inventory. As noted, this increased valuation, not representing output, is excluded from the national accounts. Changes in the value of existing assets of all types, real and financial, are excluded on the same grounds. All transactions in existing assets are excluded on both sides of the account; for corporate profits, as well as for personal income, capital gains and losses are excluded (where necessary, removed by estimation from subsidiary data that may include them). Income from existing assets—for example, interest payments—*is* included, as representing the current services performed by financial capital; similarly, rental income represents the market value of the current services performed by a rentable property.

GDP Includes Goods, Services, and Construction

The measure of output includes all forms of output—not simply tangible goods, but also creation of new construction and output of services.

The output side of the national accounts, by type of output, is shown for recent years in figure 2–3.

Output Equals Demand

The total output of the economic system is exactly equal to the total demand in the system; in fact, gross domestic product can also be referred to as gross domestic expenditure.

A moment's thought reveals that this is not a matter of divine intervention. *The holdings of inventory in the system are treated as a repository for output.* If actual **final demand** in the system were to fall short of actual output, inventories would necessarily rise, and the expenditure for inventory would be a reconciling positive number. Conversely, if final demand were to exceed output, the result would be a decline in inventory, reconciling the two aspects of the accounts. An increase in inventories is not,

Figure 2–3. Output, by Type

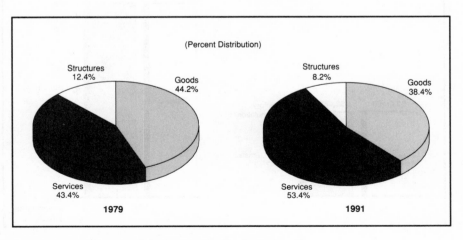

(Percent Distribution)

Structures
12.4%
Goods
44.2%
Services
43.4%
1979

Structures
8.2%
Goods
38.4%
Services
53.4%
1991

Sources: U.S. Department of Commerce; The Conference Board.

businesspersons will ruefully agree, always exactly voluntary. Whether voluntary or not, a rise in inventories is treated as a *demand* or *expenditure* for inventory; a decline in inventory is a *negative demand*. There is no inventory of services; they are consumed in the instant of their performance, and output of services always exactly equals demand. There is also no inventory of unfinished construction; the accounts pick up as fixed investment all on-site activity, whether or not the structure is finished (see figure 2–4).

Output and Demand by Sector

One way of slicing up the nation's aggregate output and expenditure is by *sector*—that is, *output and expenditure by government, by households, by business, and by our so-called international sector.*

Obviously, the identity of output and expenditure does not apply at the level of the individual sector. Only a small portion of total output is generated by households, but households take the bulk of the output off the market. It might be said that the household sector *imports* product from the other sectors. The government sector also uses up more resources than it produces. (At least, no reader will question *that*.) Conversely, business creates far more output than it consumes (both in growth of inventory and in

Figure 2–4. Output Equals Demand

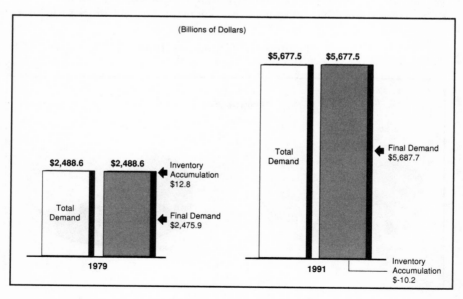

Sources: U.S. Department of Commerce; The Conference Board.

growth of its capital account); it *exports* to the other sectors. In our relations with the rest of the world, our international sector is sometimes a net exporter and sometimes a net importer. When the four sectors are added together, the identity of aggregate output and aggregate expenditure is restored. Figure 2–5 shows the output and expenditure of the sectors and of the total economy in recent years.

Total Saving Equals Total Investment

If total output equals both total expenditure and total income, then total expenditure equals total income. (You know, things equal to the same thing. . . .)

This identity applies to the economy as a whole but not to individual sectors of the economy. Typically, the consumer sector spends *less* than its income; that is, it is a net *saver.* The business sector typically spends *more* than its income; that is, it is a net *investor. Viewed this way, total saving in the economy equals total investment—an accounting identity that has many uses* (discussed later in this chapter).

Who Takes How Much of the Output

Although the aggregate is normally referred to as a product rather than an expenditure, the most frequently published structure of the accounts is by expenditure totals rather than by output totals.

The common releases on the GDP break the aggregate down into (1) the amount of GDP taken off the market by households and individuals (personal consumption expenditures); (2) the portion taken off the market by business itself (gross private domestic investment, including investment in inventory); (3) the part that, *on balance,* has been shipped abroad—exports minus imports, or *net exports;* and (4) the portion of the output taken off the market by federal, state, and local governments (government purchases). *This is the basic table in most GDP forecasts; it is the first target of the forecasting models.* The composition of these outlays, by sector, is shown for recent years in figure 2–6.

Price and Physical Output in GDP

In the usual form in which it is published, GDP is expressed in current prices—that is, the price level prevailing in the accounting period.

Thus, GDP will change as prices change and output levels change. In this form, GDP is *price × output;* every recorded change in GDP is nonspecific with respect to the measurement of change in output alone or price alone. To permit this useful separation, the U.S. Department of Commerce obligingly produces a separate measure of the change in the *physical output*

Figure 2–5. Output and Expenditure, by Sector

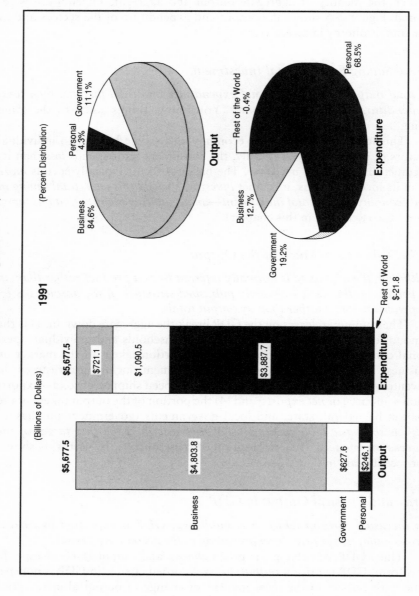

(Billions of Dollars)

1991

(Percent Distribution)

Output

$5,677.5

Business $4,803.8

Government $627.6

Personal $246.1

Expenditure

$5,677.5

$721.1

$1,090.5

$3,887.7

Rest of World $-21.8

Output

Business 84.6%

Personal 4.3%

Government 11.1%

Expenditure

Personal 68.5%

Rest of the World -0.4%

Business 12.7%

Government 19.2%

Sources: U.S. Department of Commerce; The Conference Board.

24

Figure 2–6. Who Takes How Much of the Output

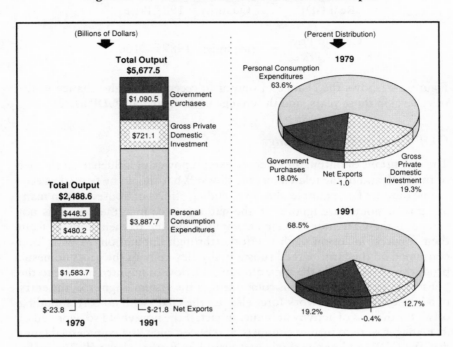

Sources: U.S. Department of Commerce; The Conference Board.

and a separate measure of the change in the *price level*. The output change describes the real growth (or decline) of the system as a whole; the change in the price index records the degree of inflation (or, very rarely indeed, deflation) of the system as a whole.

The value of GDP *before* correction for prices is often called *current-dollar GDP,* or **nominal GDP.** The GDP *after* correction for price change is called **real GDP,** or *constant-dollar GDP in 1987 prices.* The last term arises because real GDP is now constructed by pricing all output, in *all* years, at the price level prevailing in 1987, thus removing price change from any period-to-period movement in this series.

If *nominal* GDP is divided by *real* GDP, the result is an index of price change, with a base of 1987 equal to 100. Because this price index is not constructed by the usual method of combining component price indexes directly through a weighting system (as with the consumer price index), it is often called the **implicit price deflator.** The deflator is generally considered the best measure of the aggregate inflation rate.

The arithmetic of all this is as follows:

$$\frac{\text{Nominal GDP}}{\text{Real GDP}} = \frac{\text{Quantity} \times \text{Current Price}}{\text{Quantity} \times 1987 \text{ Price}} =$$

$$\frac{\text{Current Price}}{1987 \text{ Price}} = \text{Price Index}, 1987 = 100$$

Figure 2–7 shows the change in output in recent years, the change in the price level in those years, and the change in the **aggregate GDP** itself.

GDP Level and GDP Change

The *definitions* of output and income exert a powerful influence on the size of the GDP and of the related income flows. What should be treated as economic output? For example, the never-ending efforts of housewives in managing their homes are ignored in the national accounts; their work is not valued in the GDP, nor is there an imputed income to their families from their services. Inclusion of their efforts (through imputation, as with food consumed on the farm) would substantially elevate both the gross domestic product and (in exactly the same amount) the flow of imputed income to the household sector. Because this component of the system is ignored, the entry of a housewife into the work force elevates the GDP, with no corresponding offset for the loss of activity at home. In fact, if the household so deprived of its manager were to turn to commercial services, such as a commercial laundry, the GDP (and national income) would be further elevated. *The inclusiveness of the definition affects the level of the gross domestic product. But its change from year to year and quarter to quarter, resting on a consistent definition over time, is relatively free of this problem and carries a much higher significance than the actual dollar levels.*

A Necessary Statistical Note

The annual figures in the national accounts are, of course, annual totals for the specified activity or income flow—the accumulated total for the calendar year. The *quarterly* figures in the national accounts undergo two statistical processes that make them comparable to the levels of the annual data (see table 2–1).

The first of these is a *seasonal adjustment* done to all the components of the total, which corrects the particular *quarterly* figure for normal seasonal occurrences during the quarter. For example, housing-construction activity rises rapidly in the second calendar quarter of every year, not because of an actual change in conditions in the industry, but because such a rise is a normal seasonal reflection of improved weather conditions for construction activity. Similarly, sales of automobiles rise seasonally in the second quarter and sales of refrigerators and air conditioners in the third quarter. Total

Figure 2–7. Physical Output and Prices

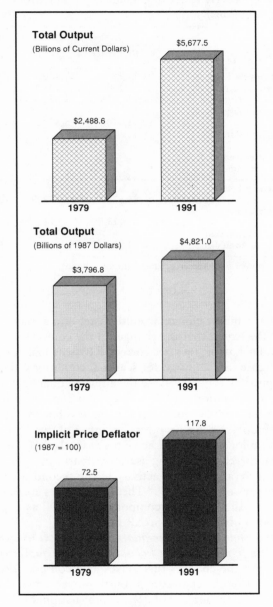

Total Output
(Billions of Current Dollars)

$5,677.5

$2,488.6

1979   1991

Total Output
(Billions of 1987 Dollars)

$4,821.0

$3,796.8

1979   1991

Implicit Price Deflator
(1987 = 100)

117.8

72.5

1979   1991

Sources: U.S. Department of Commerce; The Conference Board.

Table 2–1
Calculations of Quarterly Rates of Change in Total Output
(dollar figures in billions)

	1990 III Quarter	1990 IV Quarter	Quarterly Rates of Change	Annual Rates of Change
1. Unadjusted Quarterly Total	$1,395.0	$1,420.7		
2. Seasonal Adjustment Factor	100.2	102.3		
3. Adjusted Quarterly Total	1,392.6	1,389.4		
4. Adjusted Quarterly Total, Annualized	5,570.5	5,557.5		
5. Quarter-to-Quarter Rate of Change			−0.2%	
6. Quarter-to-Quarter Annual Rate of Change, Compounded				−0.9%
A. Adjusted Quarterly Total, Annualized	$5,570.5	$5,557.5	−0.2%	−0.9%
B. Implicit Price Deflator, 1987 = 100	113.6	114.5	+0.8%	+3.2%
C. Real (1987 Dollar) Adjusted Quarterly Total, Annualized	4,903.3	4,855.1	−1.0%	-3.9%

Sources: U.S. Department of Commerce; The Conference Board.

retail sales reach a minor climax around Easter and a major climax before Christmas. To the extent that the changes in the components simply reflect normal seasonal behavior, they are corrected by seasonal adjustment.

After the figures are adjusted for seasonal conditions, the quarterly figures are multiplied by for to elevate the adjusted quarterly totals to an *annual rate.* The abbreviation SAAR, which often appears in the headings of tables showing national-accounts data, indicates that the quarterly figures are at *seasonally adjusted annual rates.* The effect of these processes is to put the quarterly data for the national accounts at levels that are comparable to the annual data, thereby permitting useful comparisons—for example, "The annual *rate* of general economic activity in the second quarter of 1983 is back to the rate prevailing in 1979." These procedures are pursued throughout the accounts: All the output components, as well as expenditures and income flows, are published on a SAAR basis.

A percentage change from one quarter to the next in any of the SAAR national accounts figures is nevertheless still only a quarterly change. It is often useful to put the changes themselves at a *compounded annual rate,* which requires raising the change to a fourth power. From the fourth quarter of 1991 to the first quarter of 1992, total national output, in current dollars, rose by 1.4 percent; it was rising at an *annual* rate of 1.0141 to the fourth power (1.0576), or 5.8 percent. *The real growth rate in the national accounts for any quarter*—a very widely reported figure, generally taken to be an indication of how well or poorly real economic activity is progressing—is the quarter-to-quarter change in real output (adjusted for inflation), raised to the fourth power (compounded) to indicate the degree of improvement that would be achieved over an entire year if the improvement continued for four quarters at that particular quarterly rate. Similarly, the most widely reported inflation rate for the system is the quarter-to-quarter change in the *implicit price index,* raised to an annual inflation rate by compounding.

The figures in the national accounts that find their way to the general reader through the press have thus undergone a great deal of processing, but it is essentially understandable arithmetic. For the fourth quarter of 1990, for example, it was reported that the annualized real growth rate of the U.S. economy was –3.9 percent, and the inflation rate was 3.2 percent. The calculation of this figure from the raw data is shown in table 2–1.

The Measure of Output and Expenditure

The most-used table in the national accounts shows total expenditure divided by sector, and subdivided into kind of product bought. This summary table, together with far more detailed subsidiary tables in the national accounts, describes the behavior of all the markets for product categories, both in the course of the short-term business cycle and over the long term. It is basic information on the trend of business markets (see figure 2–8 and table 2–2).

Personal Consumption Expenditures

Personal consumption expenditures for durable goods, nondurable goods, and services, represent the spending—the purchasing of goods and services—of individuals and households. This is by far the largest sectoral market of the GDP, taking between sixty and sixty-five percent of all output (see figure 2–9).

Expenditures for durable goods include outlays for all goods with a presumed life of more than three years. The component labeled *automobiles and parts* includes all new passenger cars purchased during the accounting period and net acquisitions (purchases less trade-ins) of all used cars, as well as parts and accessories. Since they represent personal outlay, purchases of imported cars also appear in this category, even though they do not involve output of the U.S. economy. (This first-round overstatement of output is adjusted for in net exports, to be discussed later.) The durables category also includes all home furnishings, appliances, radio and television sets, books (but not newspapers and magazines), and even some toys. (Whoever classified toys as durable goods never had any children.) *All outlays of this sector*

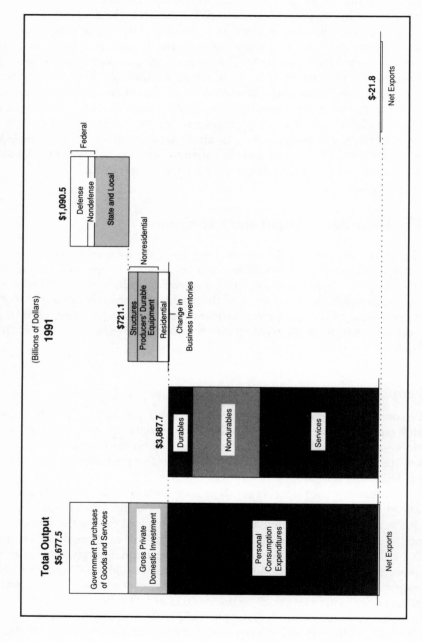

Figure 2–8. Expenditure, by Sector

(Billions of Dollars)
1991

Total Output
$5,677.5

Government Purchases of Goods and Services

Gross Private Domestic Investment

Personal Consumption Expenditures

Net Exports

$3,887.7

Durables

Nondurables

Services

$721.1

Structures

Producers' Durable Equipment

Residential

Change in Business Inventories

Nonresidential

$1,090.5

Defense

Nondefense

State and Local

Federal

$-21.8

Net Exports

Sources: U.S. Department of Commerce; The Conference Board.

Table 2–2
Gross Domestic Product Expenditures, by Sector
(billions of dollars)

	1989	1990	1991
1. Gross Domestic Product	$5,250.8	$5,522.2	$5,677.5
2. Personal Consumption Expenditures	3,523.1	3,748.4	3,887.7
3. Durables	459.4	464.3	446.1
4. Nondurables	1,149.5	1,224.5	1,251.5
5. Services	1,914.2	2,059.7	2,190.1
6. Gross Private Domestic Investment	832.3	799.5	721.1
7. Residential	230.9	215.6	190.3
8. Nonresidential	568.1	577.6	541.1
9. Structures	193.3	201.1	180.1
10. Producers' Durable Equipment	374.8	376.5	360.9
11. Change in Business Inventories	33.3	6.3	−10.2
12. Nonfarm	31.8	3.3	−10.3
13. Change in Book Value	56.6	24.5	−14.0
14. Inventory Valuation Adjustment	−24.8	−21.3	3.8
15. Farm	1.5	3.1	0.0
16. Net Exports of Goods and Services	−79.7	−68.9	−21.8
17. Exports	508.0	557.0	598.2
18. Imports	587.7	625.9	620.0
19. Government Purchases of Goods and Services	975.2	1,043.2	1,090.5
20. Federal	401.6	426.4	447.3
21. National Defense	299.9	314.0	323.8
22. Nondefense	101.7	112.4	123.6
23. State and Local	573.6	616.8	643.2

Sources: U.S. Department of Commerce; The Conference Board.

are treated as consumption, none as investment. Even an automobile, whose average life qualifies it as a depreciable investment if it is bought by a business, is defined as a consumption outlay when it is bought by an individual. This is a definitional matter; the accounts choose to restrict the term *investment* to productive facilities. There is, of course, a *stock* of long-lived consumer durables. In its flow-of-funds data (see chapter 3), the Federal Reserve even calculates an *exhaustion* or *depreciation* factor against this stock; the national accounts do not.

The purchase of nondurables by consumers includes all food and drink (consumed at home or in restaurants), all apparel, gasoline and oil for automobiles and home heating, all medical supplies, and sundries.

Figure 2–9. Personal Consumption Expenditures, by Type

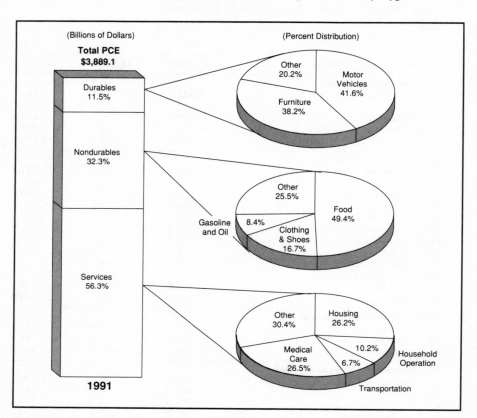

Sources: U.S. Department of Commerce; The Conference Board.

Service outlays include all services consumed by households. The largest components are rents, medical outlays, recreational service outlays, repair services, and personal care services. Personal transportation costs—air and railroad fares, fees for local transportation, and automotive repair—make up another major component. Outlays for electric, gas, and telephone utilities are treated as service expenditures.

The rental component of service outlays presents some special problems for which rather complicated solutions have been developed. For a household renting its home, no problem arises; the rent represents the services provided by the existing facility, and is included. The existence of owned homes presents a problem, however. If the rental value of these owned homes were excluded from the GDP, the GDP would rise whenever a homeowner sold a home and moved into a rental facility, and would shrink when-ever a renter acquired a home. To reflect properly the services performed by the housing stock, the national accounts estimate the rental value of owner-occupied homes, and treat that "imputed" amount as a measure of rental service purchases. Treating rent this way creates further complications on the income side of the accounts, discussed later in this chapter.

Gross Private Domestic Investment

Gross private domestic investment, the second major component of expen-diture, covers those parts of the economy that are of a private investment nature. Each word in the title is significant and necessary. The investment activities measured here are *gross* in the sense that they are *before* any de-duction for depreciation. They are *private* because the investment of govern-ment is not included. They are *domestic* because they incorporate invest-ment outlays only within the United States. They are *investment* in the ordinary business sense that they are long-lived, depreciable assets—addi-tions to balance sheets.

The figure for **residential construction** represents the value of on-site construction activity, of multiple dwellings (garden apartments and apart-ment houses), and, naturally, of single-family homes. (Mobile homes are also accounted for as residential construction, even though they are manu-factured products.) Included are all outlays during the accounting period—not just for homes and apartments completed during the period, but also for ongoing progress toward completion of structures that will be going on the market in a later accounting period. The figure is not equivalent to a sales value for residential construction; the figure picks up the outlay, whether or not the unit is sold and whether or not the unit is still in the inventory of a home builder. Because all the output of homes is represented in this figure, the national accounts do not carry an inventory of unsold residential build-ings. (Such an inventory figure is available in other data of the U.S. Depart-ment of Commerce.) The purchase of a home by a consumer is *not* a con-sumption expenditure but is treated as a business investment, putting the buyer in the business of owning a home (another complication discussed later in this chapter).

A second class of investment involves business investment in *plant and equipment.* The plant portion of this total is described in the national ac-counts as **nonresidential construction,** which includes all such structures—office buildings, manufacturing facilities, warehouses, shopping centers and other retail facilities, and so on. The machinery purchases of the business sector—called **producer durables,** as distinguished from consumer dura-bles—include outlays for all machinery for which depreciation schedules are set up; that is, all machinery and equipment with a life of three years or more. Business purchases of machinery include purchases of automobiles (about one-sixth of all cars sold annually) and trucks, and, of course, all office equipment such as computers, printers, and fax machines.

A final component of gross private domestic investment is called **change in business inventories.** For this component, some simple but special accounting arrangements are required. The intention here is to reflect the *physical increase* or *decrease* in inventories, valued at prevailing prices. At a time of rising prices, the inventories held throughout the business system tend to rise in value, even in the absence of any change in the physical stock of inventory. Ordinary dollar measures on the holdings of business inventories would thus tend to overstate the flow of output into inventory. This would not be true if all U.S. business did its accounting on the basis of LIFO (last in, first out), but a majority of firms continue to use FIFO, (first in, first out). These conditions require a correction if the inventory line of the national accounts is to treat inventory as *a repository for actual output* and if capital gains are to be excluded (as they should be) from output (see figure 2–10).

To resolve this dilemma, the U.S. Department of Commerce adjusts the dollar inventories reported to it by business for an inflation factor; that is, it converts all the inventories in the system to a LIFO basis through an **inventory valuation adjustment,** or IVA.

For example, suppose that a company holds 1,000 pounds of copper in inventory, and that its real inventory of copper is unchanged throughout an accounting period in which the market price of copper rises from 60 cents to 70 cents a pound. In the course of the accounting period, it will charge its use of copper in its operating statement at 60 cents a pound if it is on FIFO accounting, but it will be replacing its copper inventory at 70 cents a pound. The book value of its copper inventory will thus rise by 10 cents per pound, even though no *physical* change in its inventory holding has occurred. Through the inventory valuation adjustment, the U.S. Department of Commerce removes this inflation effect from its count of inventory. Since it is after not the dollar level of inventory itself, but the *change* in inventory level during the accounting period, it will report a zero change.

As with the special treatment of rental outlay, this treatment of inventory has implications for the income side of the account. *In effect, the inventory valuation adjustment becomes a measure of inventory profit on the income side of the account.* The overvaluation of inventory at the end of the accounting period represents an undercharging of business operating statements for the copper used during the accounting period. Placing business inventories on a replacement-cost basis thus reduces corporate earnings of companies accounting on a FIFO basis in a period of rising prices and raises them during periods (rare in recent history, but actually occurring in some quarters of 1986 and 1991) of falling prices (discussed later in this chapter and in chapter 3).

Figure 2–10. Accounting for Inventory Demand

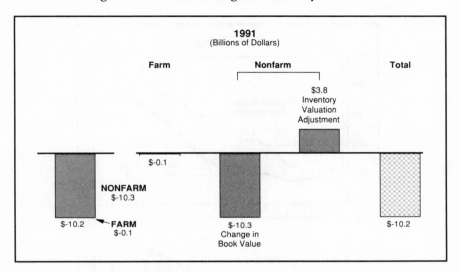

Sources: U.S. Department of Commerce; The Conference Board.

Net Exports

The next major line of the national accounts refers to **net exports.** Here, too, some simple departures from conventional business accounting are required (see figure 2–11). The term *net* in the title of the line reflects the fact that what is required is a measure of U.S. exports less imports. As an illustration, the importation and then the domestic sale of an imported automobile must be picked up in the national accounts if the expenditure totals are to be correct. When the automobile is imported and placed in the inventory of the importer, it becomes a credit to inventory (at the importer's cost); when it is sold to a consumer, the inventory account is debited for its disappearance, and consumer spending for durable goods picks it up as a credit (at its retail sale price). The value of the automobile has moved from one line of the accounts to another, but it is still reflected in the total. Since it is not part of U.S. output, and hence cannot be included in the total for GDP, a negative adjustment is required; the adjustment appears as a negative entry (at import cost) under net exports. *In other words, imports find their way into their actual market destination in the national accounts and are then removed from the total in the net export line.* The exports themselves, of course, are part of U.S. output and are properly included in the GDP.

Figure 2–11. Net Exports

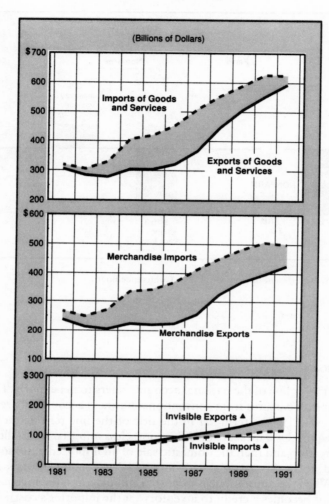

▲Services, which include mainly net tourism and net investment.
Sources: U.S. Department of Commerce; The Conference Board.

In addition to merchandise trade, the net export line must also reflect the trade in *invisibles*. Here, too, the account must be net—for example, tourism outlays of foreigners in the United States less tourism outlays of U.S. citizens abroad. The revision of the accounts structure from an ownership basis to a geographical basis affects the treatment of dividend and interest flows in the net export component. Such flows from U.S. assets abroad were formerly included in exports, and those generated by foreign-owned assets in the United States were excluded. In the conversion to GDP from GNP, receipts of foreign-earned dividends and interest are excluded from U.S. exports, while such flows generated by foreign corporations in the United States are excluded from imports. The net exports line in the national accounts is conceptually close to but not identical with the *current account balance* that appears in the balance-of-payment statistics. Actual movements of capital into and out of the country, unaccompanied by real expenditure, are transfers of assets and are not reflected in the national accounts, although they are of extreme interest to financial markets, and a powerful influence on the value of the dollar.

Government Purchases

Finally, the expenditure of *all levels of government* is a major component of the GDP (see figure 2–12). As it appears in these accounts, federal outlay is divided into national defense and nondefense, the latter category including all **government purchases of goods and services** for general government and the operations of all departments. Purchase of the services of government employees—the wage and salary payroll—is included, of course. Net increases in the inventory of crops held by the CCC (Commodity Credit Corporation) are treated as expenditures and reduction of crop inventory as sales, and, hence, as offsetting income. (The federal government runs no capital account, either within the national accounts or as a part of its own budgetary accounting system.) Outlays of state and local governments (there are about 90,000 of them) far exceed the outlays of the federal government; they account for about eleven percent of total GDP.

The government expenditures in the GDP are limited to purchases of goods and services; they exclude all so-called **transfer payments**—that is, payments made by government but not in return for goods and services. Social security payments and unemployment compensation payments are thus excluded, along with all welfare-type outlays. **Grants-in-aid to state and local governments** are excluded on the same grounds. Mainly by convention, interest payments on the federal debt are treated as transfer payments and, accordingly, are excluded from government purchases of goods and services (see the description of *total* federal budget operations later in this chapter). Expenditures of state and local governments follow the same concepts.

Figure 2–12. Government Expenditures in the National Accounts

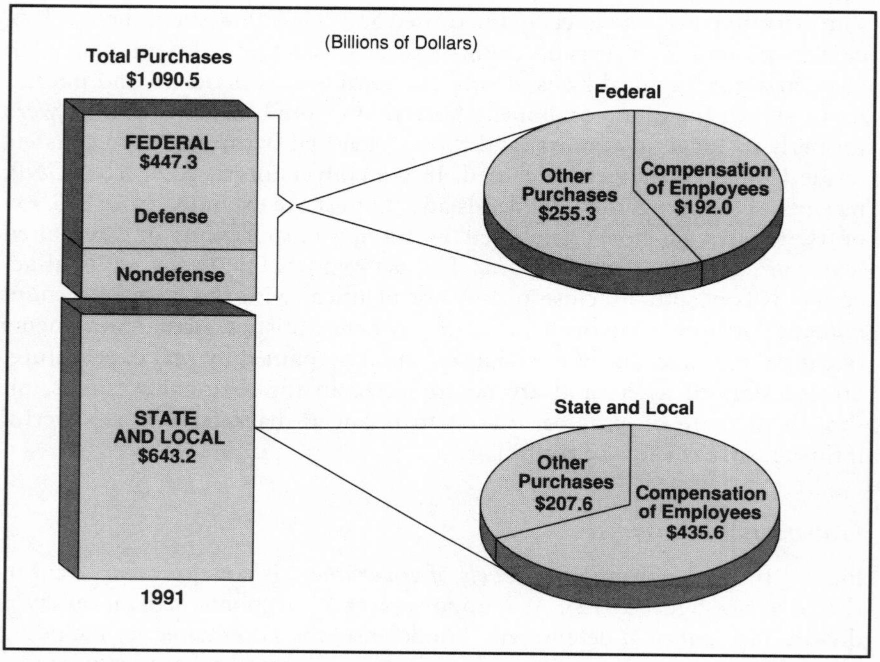

Sources: U.S. Department of Commerce; The Conference Board.

The Income Side of the Accounts

Gross domestic product measures the market value of national output. The income side of the national accounts (the national income) states the income flows generated in the course of producing the GDP—the income returns to the *factors of production* responsible for the output. These include labor and capital—capital in the fixed form of investment in plant and equipment and residential structures, as well as in the form of property and financial investments that produce rent and interest income.

National Income

The measured flows in **national income** are thus the compensation of employees; the earnings of the self-employed (both including fringe benefits, whether or not in cash); and *property incomes*—profits, rental incomes, and interest incomes. The *national income* is the sum of all these incomes, as GDP itself is the sum of all the outputs. With two important adjustments for conceptual reasons, the two totals of output and income are equal quantities, differing only by a *statistical discrepancy*—a measurement error that separates the output and income sides of the accounts.

The broad identity of the national income with the value of national output is the same old accounting truism: All the costs, including the profits that are the residual return to capital, equal the sales volume. However, some of the costs entering into the gross value of output are not really earned income to a factor of production, and the national income total, therefore, runs below the value of GDP. (A reconciliation of these series appears in table 2–3; figure 2–1 reconciles the GDP with national income.)

The depreciation flow, though not an earned income, is embedded in the gross domestic product (which is *gross,* as the reader will recall, precisely *because* it is measured *before* a deduction for depreciation). As a step in reconciling the output measure with the income side, GDP must thus be reduced by a measure of capital consumption. This produces a figure called **net national product.** One might think that such a figure would be very useful, representing as it does the flow of goods and services available to the economy *after* the replacement of the capital consumed. The measure of consumed capital is so weak, however, that the concept of net national product is rarely referred to and rarely appears in forecasts.

In addition to the adjustment for capital consumption, it is also necessary to remove from the output side of the accounts the indirect taxes—that is, sales and excise taxes levied at all levels of government. These taxes are embedded in the market value of output, but they are not an earned income flow. (The flows of general tax income to government—from corporate and personal taxes—are included in the national income, but they are not segregated; that is, the private incomes are shown *before* tax.)

These are the major adjustments required to reconcile the income side of the accounts, defined as national income, with the output side. (Two minor adjustments involve net subsidies to government enterprises and business transfers to individuals of other than earned income.)

The *national income* total is a necessary conceptual counterpart to the GDP, but it is rarely used in analysis and rarely treated in the business press when the figure is released. (Forecasters, almost without exception, simply pass it by.)

Personal Income

The measure of **personal income,** which is available monthly, is a much more effective measure of actual money flows to the personal sector—flows available for personal spending and personal saving. Personal income includes, of course, all the flows of employee compensation that appear in the national income. It also incorporates flows of transfer payments that are not earned income (and, therefore, are not reflected in national income or in the

Table 2–3

The Reconciliation of GDP with National Income and Personal Income
(billions of dollars)

			1991
1.	**Gross Domestic Product**		**$5,677.5**
2.	Plus:	Receipts of factor income from the rest of the world	143.5
3.	Less:	Payments of factor income to the rest of the world	126.0
4.	**Equals: Gross National Product**		**5,694.9**
5.	Less:	Consumption of fixed capital	626.1
6.		Capital consumption allowances	574.2
7.		Less: Capital consumption adjustment	−51.9
8.	**Equals: Net National Product**		**5,068.8**
9.	Less:	Indirect business tax and nontax equity	475.2
10.		Business transfer payments	28.1
11.		Statistical discrepancy	21.9
12.	Plus:	Subsidies less current surplus of government enterprises ..	0.5
13.	**Equals: National Income**		**4,544.2**
14.	Less:	Corporate profits with inventory valuation and capital consumption adjustments	346.3
15.		Net interest	449.5
16.		Contributions for social insurance	528.8
17.		Wage accruals less disbursements	−0.1
18.	Plus:	Personal interest income	700.6
19.		Personal dividend income	137.0
20.		Government transfer payments to persons	748.3
21.		Business transfer payments to persons	22.8
22.	**Equals: Personal Income**		**4,828.3**

Sources: U.S. Department of Commerce; The Conference Board.

GDP measure of government spending) but are, nevertheless, available for spending and saving. Furthermore, it includes only the dividend flow of income from the corporate sector; that is, it excludes the retained earnings (and the corporate tax liabilities) that are incorporated in the national income total. The monthly appearance of the personal income figure is widely reported as the best available monthly measure of incomes bearing on retail trade and consumer goods industries. Table 2–3 shows the reconciliation of personal income with national income; figure 2–13 shows the trend of various components of personal income in recent years.

Unlike national income, the resulting figure for personal income is not a pure income measure; it contains a cash flow component in the form of the transfers. It is not a pure cash flow concept either, however, since it excludes, for example, realizations of capital gains and losses in financial markets and does not reflect the borrowings or repayments of financial obliga-

Figure 2–13. Components of Personal Income

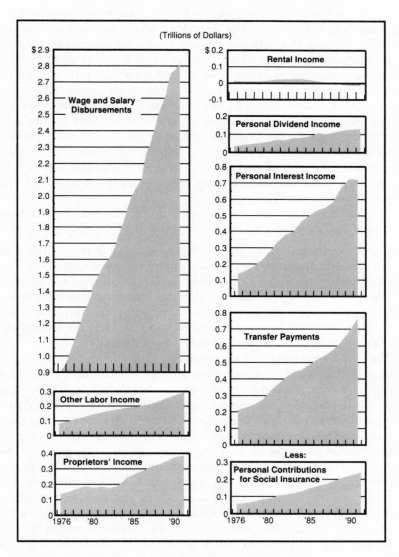

Sources: U.S. Department of Commerce; The Conference Board.

tions. Statistics on these excluded flows are broadly available, and, for analytical purposes, it is often desirable to consider them. (For example, appraisal of the actual net-worth position of the consumer sector has to give weight to the very large capital gains of the 1980s, offset by occasional immense losses, realized or unrealized, in securities and housing markets.)

Corporate Profits

The **corporate profits** account in the national income total also receives very wide attention, independently of the release of the national income totals themselves. Unlike the personal income figure, which undergoes several transformations from the total that appears in the national accounts for employee compensation, the most widely used corporate profits figures are taken directly from the national accounts, but many useful things can be done to them to increase their significance. Like all the income flows in the national income, the corporate profits figure is before taxes, but an associated figure reveals the tax liabilities against the income (in the national accounts, the corporate sector's taxes are treated on an accrual basis—that is, as the liability arises—rather than on a payment basis). The after-tax earnings are then subdivided into a component for dividend payments and a component for retained earnings.

Two further adjustments of the aggregate profits-before-taxes figures also appear in the national accounts (see figure 2–14):

1. The inventory profits resulting from appreciation of the existing stocks of corporate inventories are removed from the profits figure. It will be recalled that an inventory valuation adjustment is used to remove the effects of price change from the GDP measure of inventory change. In the GDP account, the IVA reflects adjustments for *all* inventories, including those held by unincorporated business. Here the adjustment is calculated only for inventories held by corporations.

2. The U.S. Department of Commerce estimates the presumed actual exhaustion of capital by corporations during the accounting period. If the charges to depreciation accounts by corporations fall short of the actual or true depreciation, the earnings are considered to be overstated by the inadequate provision of depreciation in the corporate operating statement, and the amount of the overstatement is removed from corporate earnings in the form of a **capital consumption adjustment (CCAdj)**. After the legislation of the accelerated cost recovery system, tax-based depreciation rose progressively above the U.S. Department of Commerce estimate of true capital exhaustion, and the Department was busily adding back the overdepreciation to corporate earnings (see figure 2–15). These adjustments convert the corporate profits figures as reported for tax purposes into a figure the U.S. Department of Commerce calls **profits from current production,** which it takes to be a true measure of the ongoing before-tax earnings from operations. In recent years, the less benevolent tax treatment of depreciation has forced tax-based depreciation deductions back to the level of true depreciation, as determined by the U.S. Department of Commerce (in its infinite wisdom. Imagine trying to calculate a "true exhaustion of capital" for the corporate sector!), and the CCAdj has returned to near zero.

Figure 2–14. Tax-Based Profits in the National Accounts

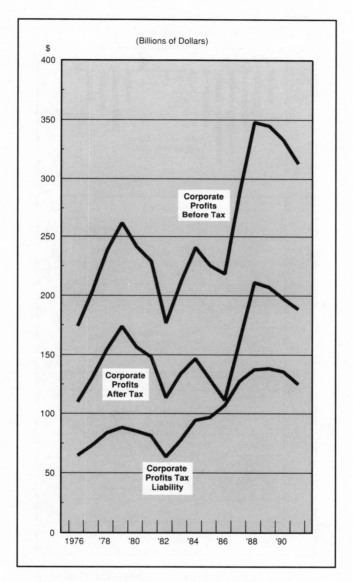

Sources: U.S. Department of Commerce; The Conference Board.

Figure 2–15. Adjustments to Corporate Profits Before Taxes

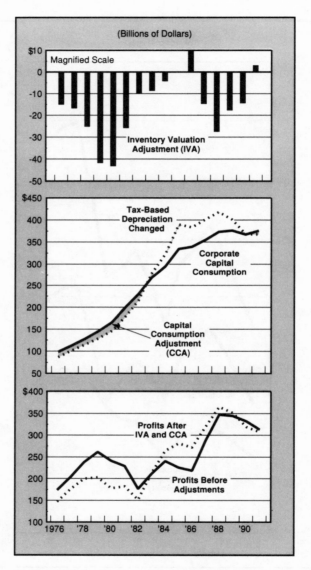

Sources: U.S. Department of Commerce; The Conference Board.

If the two adjustments are made to *after-tax* profits, the resulting adjusted series is a better measure of real earnings available for dividends and retained earnings (see figure 2–16). It should be borne in mind that the profits accounts within the national accounts, in common with all the other components, are free of all capital gains and losses.

Property Incomes and Wage Incomes

The national accounts identify a figure for compensation of employees, including supplements to wages and salaries, or *fringes*. They also identify a corporate earnings figure, the dividend component of which is a part of personal income. Additionally, the accounts identify two other property incomes—the rental income earned by persons (a later section deals with the origin of most individual rental incomes) and an interest income. In the total national income, the interest figure represents the excess of interest payments made by the business sector over the interest payments received by the business sector. The figure is thus the net return of owners of capital on their lending to the business sector, just as the dividends are the paid-out return on the equity investment in the business sector.

It is also possible and, in recent years, quite illuminating to make use of the national accounts as a way of highlighting the significance of the corporate debt burden, which grew so dramatically during the 1980s. If the interest costs confronting the corporate sector are added back to its profits, that aggregate might be called the return on investment, including the investment of bond-holder creditors, as well as the investment of the owners of the equity. The sum is the aggregate of what corporations have to distribute—to the owners of the debt in the form of interest payments, to the owners of the equity in the form of dividends, to government in the form of corporate taxes, and (again, to the holders of the equity) in the form of undistributed (or retained) earnings. Figure 2–17 shows the distribution of the return on invested capital and makes the point more clearly than does any other body of data that the earnings of shareholders in recent years have been profoundly affected by an enormous increase in the servicing required to reimburse the holders of corporate debt.

For the purposes of longer-term analysis, comparisons are often drawn between the compensation of employees, as **labor income,** and the total of dividends, interest, and rental income, as **property income** (see figure 2–18). The comparison is usable, although perhaps too much can be made of it. There is no clearly defined *labor class* or *property class* in the United States; the vast majority of households receive both kinds of income (particularly since home ownership involves a rental income).

Figure 2–16. Adjustments to Corporate Profits (After Taxes) and Retained Earnings

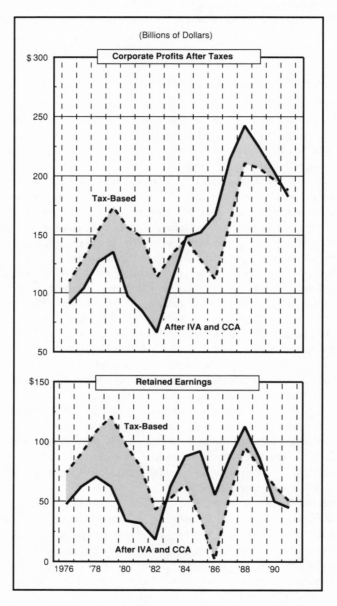

Sources: U.S. Department of Commerce; The Conference Board.

Figure 2–17. The Distribution of Earnings Before Debt Service

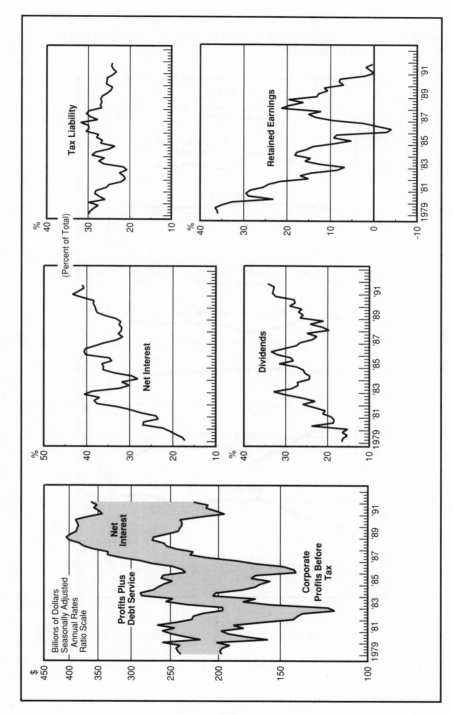

Sources: U.S. Department of Commerce; The Conference Board.

47

Figure 2–18. Labor Incomes and Property Incomes as a Percentage of National Income

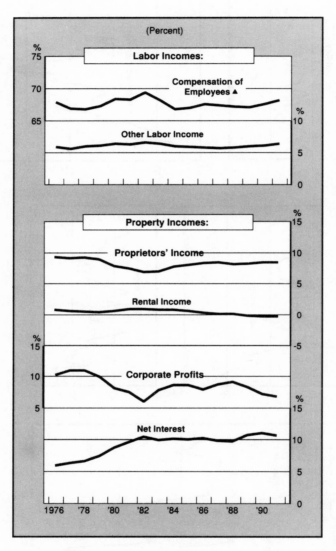

▲Excluding "Other Labor Income."
Sources: U.S. Department of Commerce; The Conference Board.

Relations Between the Output and Income Sides of the Accounts

The national accounts describe an accounting entity that produces output and income and then proceeds to use the income to consume virtually all of its own output. Relating components of the output side of the system to the income side produces some of the most useful analysis available in the national accounts. It also produces some accounting complexities that are not present in normal business accounting.

Personal Income, Spending, and Saving

The components of the national accounts that bear on the behavior of the personal sector produce by-products that are of great significance to all business, but particularly to the consumer goods industries and retailers, whose activities represent nearly two-thirds of the total economy.

If personal income is reduced by the tax burden of individuals levied against them by all governments, the resulting figure is the famous **disposable personal income**—that is, income available after taxes. If the *spending* of individuals is subtracted from this figure, and if we also remove the interest payments of individuals (excluding payments on residential mortgage interest) and certain transfers from the individual sector to other sectors of the accounts (for example, the transfer of funds to relatives abroad), the resulting figure—now only a small fraction of the personal income with which this sector of the accounts begins—is, conceptually, **personal saving.**

This saving figure, available quarterly in the national accounts, both as a dollar amount and as a percentage of disposable income, is widely, if a little uneasily, regarded as a measure of the saving propensity of the U.S. consumer and of the U.S. personal sector as a whole. The percentage figure, historically, has run at five to six percent of income, but it has recently been erratic and abnormally low. As might be expected, the figure tends to rise in any quarter in which a tax reduction suddenly becomes effective, as it did in the third quarters of 1981, 1982, and 1983. Thereafter, it appears to settle gradually back again, as the increase in disposable income resulting from a tax reduction gradually finds its way into the spending stream.

Other important cautions about the personal saving figure are in order. In the first place, it is statistically very volatile because it is measured as a lumpy, undifferentiated aggregate—simply the subtraction of one very large number (personal consumption expenditures) from another very large number (disposable personal income). Even small percentage errors in the measurement of one or both of these large aggregates produce disproportionately large errors in the personal saving rate. Additionally, the saving rate shares with the rest of the national accounts the exclusion of all income flows resulting from capital gains and losses; there have been years in which these gains and losses (predominantly in the changing value of financial assets) have had a dramatic impact on the financial condition of the personal sector. The saving rate misses all the accumulated capital gains (and, more recently, losses) in holdings of residential real estate.

Finally, the saving concept here is so broad that it is difficult to interpret. Because of the conceptual structure of the two aggregates whose difference it represents, the saving figure is enormously inclusive. It covers all net saving in financial forms (increases in net new saving but not capital gains on existing holdings), as well as saving in physical forms (net acquisition of equity in residential property), as well as net increase in the cash value of insurance reserves (in general, the premium payments less expenses of the insurance companies—including their profits, if they are not mutual companies). It includes all increases in pension reserves, and it reflects the activities of unincorporated businesses (discussed later). Other figures outside the framework of the national accounts can be used to resolve this gross aggregate into its components— particularly the resolution into *financial saving* less increase in financial liabilities, and *saving in tangible assets* less the applicable depreciation.

Despite the awkwardness of the measure, it is widely used, particularly in international comparisons. The figure is often said to indicate that the U.S. personal saving rate is low relative to the prevailing rates in many other countries—most strikingly, West Germany and Japan. The implication is that the United States, in its present stage, is a high-consumption, low-saving society (see figure 2–19), a condition whose origin and present importance were described in chapter 1 and will be returned to in chapter 8 on the U.S. future.

Unincorporated Business in the National Accounts

For some obvious reasons, it is difficult to deal with the huge and diversified **unincorporated business** sector in the national accounts. A corporation is an accounting entity. The accounting shield around it identifies its income as a corporate income (not the income of the shareholders who own the corporation), and it is treated as a taxable entity by the federal tax structure. The unincorporated business, on the other hand, has neither an accounting nor a legal shield protecting its income and assets. It is obvious enough that the income drawn from an unincorporated business by its owner is personal income to the owner—as are, of course, the wage and salary payments to employees of unincorporated business. But what can be done about changes in the net worth of the unincorporated enterprise?

On the income side, the national accounts do not segregate unincorporated business from the personal sector. Personal income thus includes all proprietors' income, plus the increase in the net worth of the unincorporated

Figure 2–19. International Comparisons of Personal Saving Rates

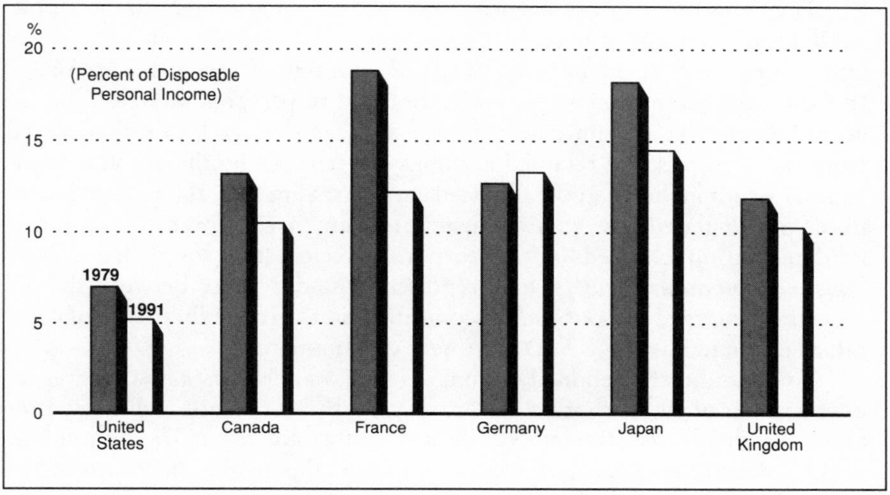

Sources: Organization for Economic Cooperation and Development; The Conference Board.

enterprise. Since the increase in net worth is not expended on consumer goods, all of this element of personal income moves into the measure of saving. The somewhat strange result is that personal saving reflects increases in the capital assets (after depreciation) and inventories of unincorporated enterprises.

On the expenditure side, the *purchases* of unincorporated enterprises appear in the gross domestic account in the appropriate categories; that is, their purchases of all business equipment appear in the nonresidential construction and producer durables categories, and the change in their inventory position is a component of the change in business inventories. The treatment of unincorporated business in the accounts thus straddles the personal sector and the business sector; the income side is in the personal sector, the expenditures in the business sector. Only a great deal of processing can reveal the relations among income, spending, and saving for these businesses; in any event, the issue rarely arises in general analysis and forecasting.

Aggregate Business Income and Investment

On the output side of the national accounts, the purchases of all business (corporate and unincorporated) consist of all the components of gross private domestic investment—the outlays for plant and equipment by all business and outlays for net additions to inventory (a net reduction of inventory is a negative entry, a partial disinvestment). All residential construction is also a business outlay, even though it may end up in the household sector (discussed later in this chapter).

The definition of **business gross income** in the national accounts applicable to this concept of business expenditure is necessarily somewhat fuzzy and complicated. It includes the retained earnings of the corporate sector (the dividend payments are properly allocated to personal income). But, in accordance with the requirement that all capital gains and losses be removed from the accounts, the retained earnings are reduced by the amount of inventory profit included in the reported earnings. Similarly, the retained earnings so calculated are then adjusted for any overdepreciation or underdepreciation charged in the corporate sector (the so- called *capital consumption adjustment*), which represents the difference between the depreciation charged in tax-based accounting and the true exhaustion of capital, as estimated by the U.S. Department of Commerce.

To this adjusted retained earnings figure is added the actual aggregate depreciation of the corporate sector, to yield the corporate cash flow after taxes and dividends. (Remember, these accounts are *gross*. The output side is not reduced for exhaustion of capital; hence, the income side must incorporate the depreciation flow.)

Finally, a **depreciation allowance** for all noncorporate business must be added to business gross income. This figure includes all depreciation of capital facilities owned by unincorporated business, including farms. Since home ownership is treated as a business in the national accounts (that is why residential building is treated as an investment component), a depreciation flow against all residential building facilities is also included in the business cash flow.

That is the business sector in the national accounts. Though not conceptually beautiful, it is the best that can be done given two factors: the difficulty in treating unincorporated business as having one foot in the personal sector and one foot in the business sector; and the need to treat home ownership as a business activity.

The results are, nevertheless, coherent. As would be expected, the business sector is the characteristic investing sector for the system as a whole. The personal sector saves, on balance; the business sector invests, on balance. Figure 2–20 shows the expenditure of the business sector and its income; the characteristic gap is net business expenditure, or net investment of the business sector.

Housing in the National Accounts

The treatment of **home ownership** in the national accounts illustrates the kinds of special problems that distinguish national accounting from conventional business accounting. In the national accounts, it would be unfortunate

Figure 2–20. Business Income and Investment

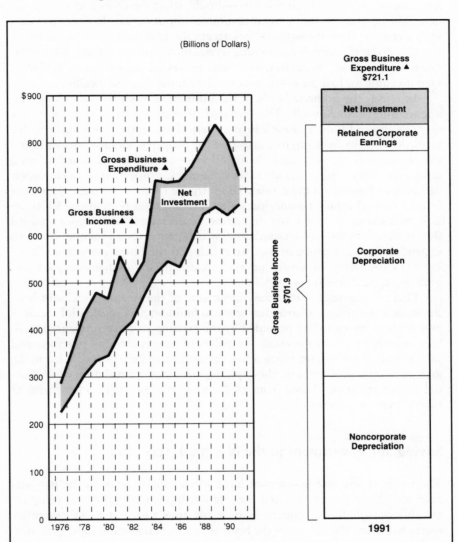

▲▲Retained Corporate Earnings plus Corporate and Noncorporate Depreciation (or Gross Private Saving less Personal Saving).

Sources: U.S. Department of Commerce; The Conference Board.

if a simple change in the legal status of an occupied dwelling—that is, from a rent status to an ownership status—should affect the gross domestic product, since no real change in any measurable output occurs. In order to avoid such a change, the national accounts accept the rental cost of a rented property as a dollar measure of the housing service the property provides. For owner-occupied dwellings, the accounts estimate the rental value of an owner-occupied dwelling and all the costs associated with owning the dwelling.

In effect, the homeowner is in the business of owning a dwelling unit and renting it to himself. The *imputed* or estimated rental value is the owner's expenditure, included in personal consumption expenditures for services. The income from ownership of the property, included under rental income in personal income, is the rental value (which is consumed in kind) minus the costs, which include real estate taxes, property insurance, depreciation, and interest on the residential mortgage (if any). In recent years, the imputed rental value of owner-occupied dwellings has been about $400 billion, and the associated costs (including depreciation) have about equaled that figure. It is an odd arrangement, which generates an income flow, an expenditure, and a profit or loss from being in the home-owning business; but it is necessary to assure parallel treatment for owner-occupied and renter-occupied dwellings.

One consequence is that the output side of the accounts includes both the value of ongoing construction work in building new residential facilities and the occupancy values provided by the existing stock of residential facilities (whether rented or owned). Transfers of homes through purchase and sale do not, of course, represent a form of output and are not included in the gross domestic product; and the capital gains from appreciation of residential real estate are excluded from all the accounts, as are all other forms of capital gains and losses.

Saving and Investment in the National Accounts

The terms **saving and investment** have special significance in the national accounts. Their definitions, and the relationship between them, develop inevitably out of the accounting system; but they turn out to be extremely useful in tracing the history of the business cycle, in understanding its causes, and in forecasting its future course.

It will be recalled that for the system as a whole, total output, total expenditure, and total income are equal quantities. If certain expenditures are designated *consumption* and the remainder are designated *investment,* then it follows that saving equals total income minus consumption, and investment is total output minus consumption. *Given the equality of income and output, it follows that saving equals investment, no matter how consumption is defined.*

The accounts, in fact, define consumption as consisting of all personal spending, even such consumer-durables categories as automobiles, appliances, home furnishings, and other durable goods; and all outlays of government, whether they are for durable goods, construction, payroll, or crop inventory. The investment side of this definition includes all business expenditures—for housing, nonresidential construction, producer durables, and net change in inventory—in other words, gross private domestic investment. Also included as investment are net exports; when net exports are negative (that is, when the United States is running an import surplus) this becomes a negative entry on the investment side of the system, or disinvestment.

The saving flows that equal the investment flows consist of the personal saving done in the personal sector, the retained earnings and depreciation of the business sector (including depreciation flows on homes), and the surplus of the government sector (a government deficit is *negative* saving, or dissaving). The depreciation flows need to be included, since these are gross accounts, seeking a gross saving estimate. Table 2–4 shows the identity of the two sides of the account, with a minor "statistical discrepancy" (an exquisitely dignified term for error).

For the total system, then, saving and investment are almost interchangeable terms; they are an accounting identity. *For any accounting period, aggregate saving will equal aggregate investment, apart from errors of measurement.*

However, just as the identity of sources and uses of funds in a corporate statement applies only to the total business entity and not to its divisions or subsidiaries, so in the national accounts the saving-investment identity prevails for the entire economy, but not for the individual sectors. Only when the sectors are added together is the identity achieved.

The personal sector is generally a large net saver; its income exceeds its outlay, and the balance is referred to as net personal saving. The business sector is characteristically a net investor; that is, it spends more on construction, machinery, and inventories than its gross cash flow from earnings and depreciation. The government sector may be a saver (when it runs a surplus) or a dissaver or investor, if its expenditures exceed its income. The international sector may be a net investor when it is running a surplus or a disinvestor when it is running a deficit. The historical behavior of each of the sectors is shown in figure 2–21.

There is, of course, no reason at all why the intentions of savers and investors *at the beginning of an accounting period* should reflect such an identity. For example, if consumers are particularly confident of the future and have strong propensities to spend, they may wish to increase their spending and *save less.* At the same time, the business sector, perhaps encouraged by the same underlying conditions, may wish to *invest more.* Of this situation, it is said that the *ex ante* (before-the-fact) intentions to save and invest are *not* in balance; there is an excess of intention to invest.

Table 2–4
Gross Saving
(billions of dollars)

		1981	1991
1.	GROSS SAVING	$557.2	$708.2
2.	GROSS PRIVATE SAVING	586.4	901.5
3.	Personal saving	192.4	199.6
4.	Undistributed corporate profits with inventory valuation and capital consumption adjustments	31.7	75.8
5.	Undistributed profits	78.6	64.2
6.	Inventory valuation adjustment	−25.7	3.1
7.	Capital consumption adjustment	−21.2	8.4
8.	Corporate consumption of fixed capital	219.4	383.0
9.	Noncorporate consumption of fixed capital	143.0	243.1
10.	Wage accruals less disbursements	0.0	0.0
11.	Government Surplus or Deficit (−), National Income and Product Accounts	−30.3	−193.3
12.	Federal	−58.8	−210.4
13.	State and local	28.5	17.1
14.	Capital Grants Received by the United States (net)	1.1	0.0
15.	GROSS INVESTMENT	568.1	730.1
16.	Gross private domestic investment	558.0	721.1
17.	Net foreign investment	10.1	9.0
18.	Statistical Discrepancy	10.9	21.9

Sources: U.S. Department of Commerce; The Conference Board.

If we examine the consequences of this imbalance, we can appreciate the influence of these abstruse calculations, so far from ordinary marketplace reality. In the real world, consumers will, in effect, be bidding for such material resources as steel (which enters into automobiles and appliances) at the same time that the business sector is bidding for steel (for plant construction, machinery, and perhaps to build up inventories of steel); and steel production will accordingly rise. The same condition will prevail for a host of other goods and services, including labor itself. *An excess of investing intentions over saving intentions thus carries the suggestion of an expanding economy. Conversely, an excess of saving intentions over investing intentions connotes a falling economy—that is, a level of aggregate demand inadequate to support current production.*

In response to these forces, the resulting movement of the economy itself eliminates the *ex ante* imbalance. During an expansion, consumer incomes rise, tending to elevate their saving, and government revenues rise (as taxable incomes rise), tending to reduce its deficit (dissaving); the reverse happens in a recession. *When we look back on any accounting period, the* ex ante *differences have been obliterated in these and other ways by the behav-*

Figure 2–21. Saving and Investment, by Sectors

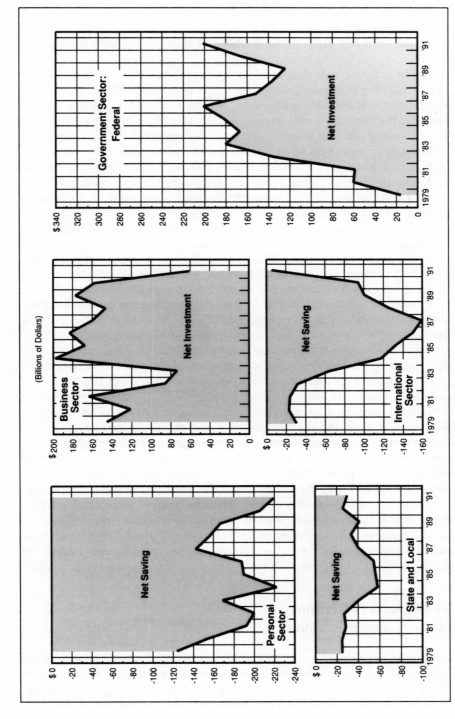

Sources: U.S. Department of Commerce; The Conference Board.

57

ior of the economy itself. An *ex post*—after-the-fact—identity has been restored.

In forecasting, it is useful to know where the *ex ante* intentions stand. The forecasting profession, accordingly, has developed a large array of surveys of spending and saving intentions of consumers and businesses to get at precisely that issue (see also chapter 4). A budget projection by the federal government, indicating whether and to what degree it will run a surplus or a deficit, is a projection of the saving (or dissaving) intentions of government, which accounts for the significance attached to the budget projections by forecasters. Other things being equal, a budget deficit, being an investment (dissaving) intention, is stimulative to the business system; a surplus (a saving intention) is restrictive.

A last, unfortunately rather abstruse, note is required. The identity of saving and investment in the national accounts applies to real saving—real in the sense of a withholding of current income from consumption. It does not reflect the increases in financial wealth that may result from increases in the value of existing and tangible assets. And it does not reflect *creation* of new credit, of which the Federal Reserve and the commercial banking system are superbly capable (see chapter 5). The value of the financial assets in the system, therefore, may rise faster than would be indicated by the real saving out of income. If the Federal Reserve *monetizes* the federal debt—that is, if it arranges to lend to the federal government through its own purchases of government securities or through its powers to enlarge the lending of commercial banks by increasing their reserve positions—then the real saving is being supplemented by created financial resources. Monetarists stress that this creation of financial resources over and above the real saving of the system is the ultimate source of inflation. According to this reasoning, it is not the budget deficit itself that is inflationary; it is the creation of financial wealth over and above the real saving rate, as the Federal Reserve contributes to the financing of the deficit, that is the true cause of inflation, because it violates the *ex post* identity of saving and investment. In this respect, as in many others, the real world departs from the conceptual world of the national accounts. Forecasters accordingly pay a great deal of attention to the political and economic forces that operate on the federal budget and on the Federal Reserve's behavior with respect to the creation of money and credit.

The Federal Government in the National Accounts

Within the conceptual framework of the national accounts, there is an accounting of **federal government receipts, expenditures,** and **surplus or deficit** that very largely mirrors the actual budget of the federal government, as legislated by the Congress and experienced by the Department of the Treasury. The conceptual differences between the two sets of accounts are not really substantial; there are some differences in timing (that is, some accounts are picked up on an accrual basis rather than on the cash basis used in the federal budget) and minor differences in coverage. On the whole, what happens to the budget legislated by the Congress is accurately reflected in the federal government sector of the national accounts. The national accounts have a big advantage, however; the federal sector's operations are available quarterly at seasonally adjusted annual rates, and they can be compiled into calendar-year annual data comparable to the data available for all the other sectors. (The legislated budget is on a September 30 fiscal year.) The national accounts version of the federal budget is a preferred statistical device for integrating the federal government's operations into a forecast.

As reflected in the national accounts, the receipts of the federal government include all personal tax receipts, corporate profits tax accruals, and indirect business tax receipts—excise taxes and customs duties. They also include receipts of the social insurance funds. Expenditures include all purchases of goods and services and all transfer payments, as well as grants-in-aid to state and local governments, the net interest paid (interest payments minus interest receipts), and the net subsidies of the federal government to government enterprises (subsidies less the current surpluses of government enterprises). If the expenditures are subtracted from the receipts, the resulting surplus or deficit closely parallels the budget operations recorded in the government's actual balance or receipts and expenditures on an *annual* basis; but quarterly comparisons are complicated by the immense seasonal patterns in budget receipts, which are not available on a seasonally adjusted basis. The national income version of the federal budget appears in figure 2–22. Forecasts of the national accounts thus generally produce usable forecasts, or at least insights, concerning the future budget position of the federal government implied by the general business forecast and, hence, some insight into the policy issues ahead.

Long-Term Trends in the National Accounts

The statistical record of the GDP goes back over four decades, with nearly perfect conceptual consistency; with only modest conceptual change, the series goes back to 1929. (Even earlier data, but with considerable conceptual inconsistency, go back to the turn of the century.) The long-term record of the accounts makes only a minor direct contribution to short-term forecasting; but longer-term projections of where the economy will be ten years, or even only five years, in the future properly draw on the long historical record as the basis for calculating normal or expectable growth. These long-term projections are an attempt to ignore the business cycle; that is, they deal with a period in which recessions and expansions might be expected to cancel

Figure 2–22. The Federal Budget in the National Accounts

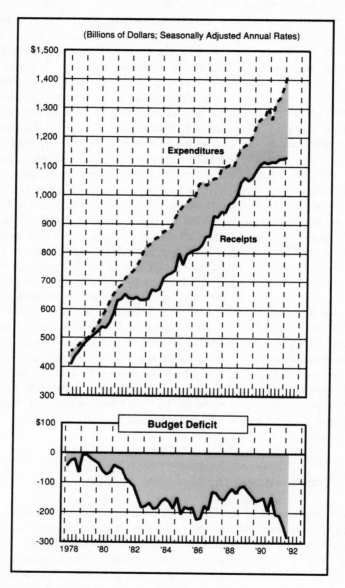

Sources: U.S. Department of Commerce; The Conference Board.

out, revealing long-term movements dominated by underlying conditions of growth rather than of a cyclical nature.

Since price forecasting is uncertain and difficult even over the long term, projections of the national economy that run beyond the ordinary forecasting concerns of the business cycle tend to deal with the real (inflation-adjusted) GDP as the available reality. As illustration of uses for long-term accounts, figure 2–23 compares the U.S. growth rate, in terms of inflation-adjusted GDP, with the growth rates being experienced by the more important of our Western trading partners, as calculated from their own generally comparable data.

Actual and Middle-Expansion Trend Output

A recent extension of national accounting seeks to describe the course of our real *potential* for producing the GDP—that is, the resources of capital facilities and manpower that are the real inputs. The **middle-expansion,** or **cyclically adjusted,** trend of **output** (formerly called the *high-employment* GDP), shown in figure 2–24, is a description of our supposed economic potential. Charted with it is our actual output—the degree to which we have achieved the potential; the gap between the two lines charted, also shown as a per-

Figure 2–23. GDP/GNP Growth, Here and Abroad

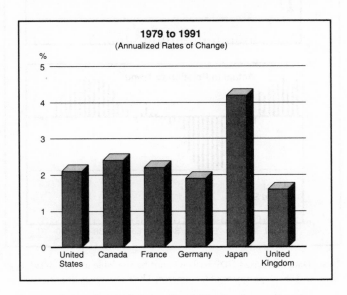

Sources: International Monetary Fund; The Conference Board.

Figure 2–24. Actual and Middle-Expansion Trend Output

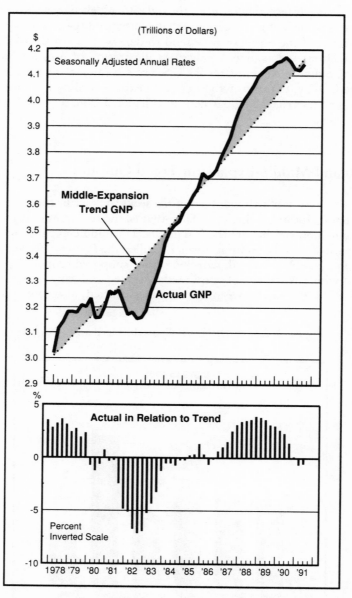

Note: Data on revised GDP basis will not be available until mid-1993.
Sources: U.S. Department of Commerce; The Conference Board.

centage of our potential, represents our shortfall from the potential. There is no single, ordained, cyclically adjusted GDP; rather, several versions of it are calculated (by the U.S. Department of Commerce and others). The differences among such series will reflect differences in judgment about which unemployment rate should be associated with the concept of *long-term trend*, as well as what kind of productivity gain should be assumed in the long-term trajectory of output.

It is generally accepted that as the system's output falls away from its high-employment potential, the resources thus made idle compete with the resources in use and tend to arrest inflation. Conversely, as actual output begins to approach the potential closely, the idle resources shrink, competition for supply increases, and the inflation rate tends to rise. These propositions are often related to conventional business cycle propositions about inflation; that is, an accelerating business recovery would normally strengthen prices, whereas recession would weaken them. In some periods—1983 is a good illustration—the two sets of reasoning about inflation tend to be offsetting; a very vigorous recovery with implicit price consequences occurred at a time when the economy was still experiencing a substantial shortfall from high employment. Similar, but not as dramatic, circumstances have prevailed in the early 1990s. These considerations have been clearly reflected in discussions of inflation prospects in 1992: moderately growing markets, but still abundantly available supply.

From 1983 to 1987, the growth of markets slowed, and a much larger share of demand in the United States was served by imports; that is, U.S. markets for goods grew more rapidly than U.S. production of goods. In the late 1980s, and continuing into the first years of the new decade, exports have grown faster than imports; U.S. production has accordingly risen faster than domestic demand. These propositions, drawn from the national accounts, provide a useful way of looking at the complicated problems faced by the Federal Reserve—whether or not to restrain a vigorous recovery for fear of inflation, even while the volume of idle resources remains substantial. In these and manifold other uses, the national accounts continue to play a central role in debates about the state of business and the suitability of existing or proposed policies of the federal government.

3

The Data Stream

Standing behind the national accounts, and contributing the raw materials from which the national accounts are produced, is a nearly infinite stream of data—almost all of it issued monthly, and almost all of it reported with interest in the business press. These are the figures that make the short-term news; they give business journalism its raw materials and its daily excitement. Any inclusive compilation of this Niagara of data would make a formidable reference work; indeed, the U.S. Department of Commerce publishes, biennially, an oversized two-hundred-page volume of such data that is itself incomplete, even though it goes far beyond the needs of a sophisticated observer intent on watching major developments in the U.S. business system.

What follows here is a highly selective collection of the principal indicators that make the news, and that nudge economic opinion in one direction or another. The statistics described here are organized by sector. A ruthless selection process has driven the number of series (and even the number of sectors) down to what we can all hope to grasp and retain, so that when the next release in the series is reported in the business press, it will be recognized and understood for what it is. Series whose principal bearing is on the behavior of the business cycle or on the functioning of economic policy are reserved for later chapters. Here, we are after the raw materials of economic appraisal—the staccato reporting of a small number of very important figures that shed their light each time they appear, and then disappear from the news until their next release a month later. Typical monthly and quarterly calendars of statistical reports, showing their approximate dates of release and the compiling source, appear in appendices B and C.

The Personal Sector:
Income, Spending, Credit Use

The personal sector buys about two-thirds of total national output—easily the dominant component of U.S. business. About half of all the personal spending is for *services,* a varied and elusive outlay that runs all the way from rents to haircuts. Far more interesting, from a general analytic viewpoint, is the expenditure rate on goods at retail—a figure covered by a retail sales release published by the U.S. Department of Commerce on about the thirteenth day of every month, covering all retail volume in the preceding month.

The **retail sales** figure is broken down into durable goods (those that presumably last three years or more) and nondurable goods (everything else, including food, clothing and shoes, gasoline and oil, and other miscellaneous softgoods). The principal interest attaches to the sales of durable goods and, most particularly, of motor vehicles and parts, which account for about half of all durable goods.

Figure 3–1 shows the recent composition of aggregate retail volume. The monthly data are seasonally adjusted, but not adjusted for inflation. This is dollar volume at the nation's retail counters. The sales volume of automotive dealers (including the gross volume of used-car sales), of retail outlets for durable goods other than automobiles, and of several types of softgoods outlets are shown separately. General merchandise stores, which may sell durables as well as softgoods, are classified in the softgoods; the classification is by type of store, not by type of merchandise. Each monthly release revises the figure for the preceding month; the revisions (based on more complete data) are often very large; the tentative early releases must be taken with several teaspoons of caution.

Among the important influences affecting the current and prospective volume of retail trade are the rate of growth of personal income (a component of the quarterly national accounts but produced by the U.S. Department of Commerce monthly); the psychological attitudes of consumers; and the use of consumer credit, particularly to finance big-ticket durable goods.

The monthly figure on personal income is an inclusive measure of the flow of income to households and is thus a major indicator of the probable trend of retail markets. It is a broad figure that moves smoothly over the short term; sharp changes in retail spending occur even while the income flow maintains a steady trend.

Analysis of the surveys of **consumer attitudes** (done not by the government, but by such private nonprofit institutions as The Conference Board and the University of Michigan) reveals no close, short-term correspondence with current retail volume; but a prolonged rise or decline in sentiment, sustained over several months, has large and obvious significance.. Some of the surveys of consumer attitudes also report on the buying plans of consumers. These series are highly volatile and have little short-term application (see figure 3–2).

The statistics on use of **consumer credit** are compiled by the Federal Reserve and are issued about thirty days after the month to which they apply. They include estimates of the total amount of credit outstanding by type—installment credit for automobiles and other durables purchases and

Figure 3–1. The Composition of Retail Volume

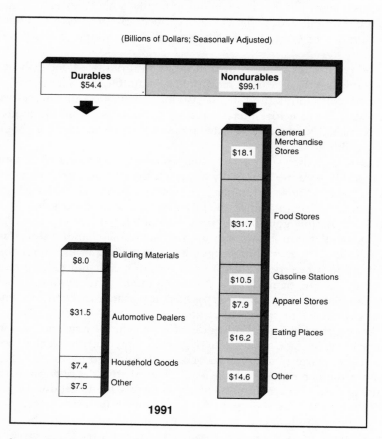

Sources: U.S. Department of Commerce; The Conference Board.

personal (unsecured) loans. This is *short-term* credit; mortgage credit is not included. In addition to the amount outstanding, the releases used to include measures of the rate of *new* credit extension and repayment, but these very useful series were abandoned in one of the budget crises that periodically beset the statistical agencies in Washington. Credit use by consumers seems to be a violent cyclical accompaniment to retail trade; its volume, in terms of net increase in debt outstanding, oscillates dramatically with general business conditions and parallels the behavior of the automobile market, to which much of installment credit is directed.

Beginning in 1987, the tax deductibility of interest on installment credit entered on a swift phase-out. Consumer borrowing has accordingly shifted to debt on residential property—the **home equity loan,** apparently beloved

Figure 3–2. Consumer Attitudes and the Use of Credit

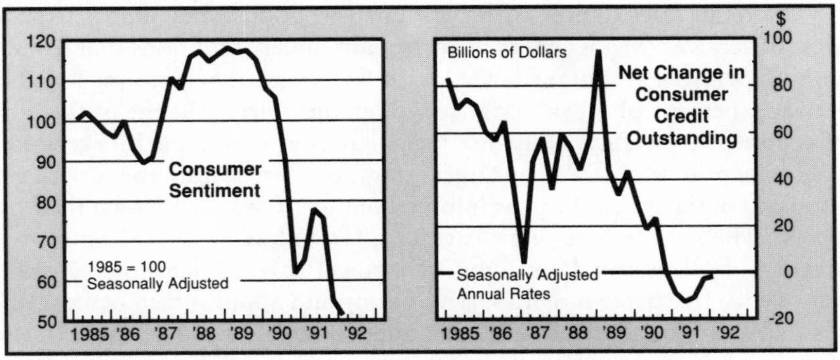

Sources: Federal Reserve; The Conference Board.

by borrower and lender alike. Interest payments on such loans are relatively low and, in the main, deductible; and there is more than one trillion dollars of as yet unmortgaged equity available. The sudden birth and awesome growth of such debt is not yet the subject of a separate statistical series, but never fear, it will be. At this writing, the outstanding volume is closing in on $100 billion. It may be worth remembering that thirty-seven percent of all U.S. families do not own their own homes and have no equity to mortgage. Such lost souls are still dependent on installment credit, with its higher rates, shorter terms, and lost deductibility.

The automobile industry releases figures on sales of domestic models for periods covering ten days of sales—that is, three times a month (the figures are seasonally adjusted by the U.S. Department of Commerce, as well as by private agencies). The production rate for the domestic automobile industry is reported every month in "Ward's Automotive Reports," an industry trade publication, along with figures on dealer inventories and the prices of used cars. An automobile purchase shows the U.S. consumer in his most revealing moment, reconciling his desires with his finances and his sense of job security. Automobile sales are thus a dominant (but highly variable) influence on impressions of the strength or weakness of retail sales. A strong automobile trend is seldom contradicted by the rest of the retail market, but there are tricks to even this seemingly simple statistic; for example, highly erratic sales to rental companies (which are treated as a business purchase, not a personal outlay).

Retail sales are reported in seasonally adjusted dollar amounts, with no adjustment for inflation. Of course, the figures can be "corrected" for inflation by dividing them by a suitable price index (the consumer price index, or some selection from it, would be the natural choice). But a good general rule for reading statistics is the less processing the better; each process removes the numbers further from reality. It's often best to stay with the dollar numbers, viewed intuitively with respect to the effects of inflation.

The retail sales figures stick with tangible goods; they ignore expenditures for services even where they are bought under conditions that simulate "retail." Services are, nevertheless, hard to ignore; they account for about forty-five percent of all personal spending and thirty percent of the entire gross domestic product. Only quarterly figures are available for services, as a component in the GDP. The largest single account within the service total is housing outlay (including the imputed outlay of those who own their own homes). The next largest single category, far and away the fastest growing category of all personal spending, is medical care, which now represents over twenty-five percent of all service outlay and about fifteen percent of all personal spending. Other major categories are household operation (including utilities) and transportation. As a group, service outlays experience a substantial upward drift; they exhibit very little sensitivity to changes in general economic conditions.

The Housing Market

Housing construction and sale is a deceptively small component of the total system; residential construction activity accounts for only about four percent of total national output. It is a highly volatile industry, however, and the violent waves—business cycles—in the housing industry are transmitted down the line to such major industries as forest products, nonferrous metals, and fabricated construction materials and supplies.

The basic statistic on activity in the housing industry, as shown in figure 3–3, relates to **housing units started;** the release is called "Housing Starts," and is published by the U.S. Department of Commerce in the middle of each month, covering activity in the preceding month. A *housing start* refers to the breaking of ground—the actual commencement of construction. The starts figures are available for single-family dwellings and for multiple (apartment house) structures (each apartment of which is considered a start). In addition to starts, the U.S. Department of Commerce also collects the rate of building-permit issuance, a figure that is assumed to lead starts by a month or more. Figures are also available from the same source on units completed (with an average lag from start to completion of about three months) and on both new and existing homes sold and for sale. Commerce also provides monthly figures on the vacancy rate in rental units. Theoretically, these numbers should be very useful in appraising the future of the market, but the market itself does not ordinarily seem to be sensitive to vacancies, and they are rarely consulted.

The housing market is, by its nature, a collection of regional markets. The U.S. Department of Commerce accordingly publishes considerable re-

Figure 3–3. The Housing Industry: Starts and Building Permits

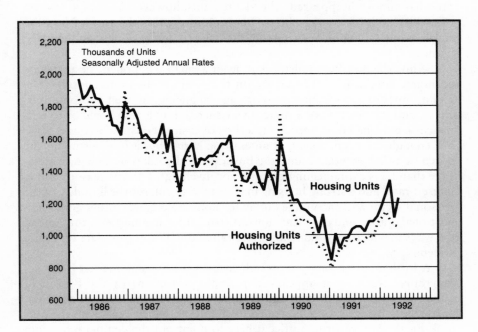

Sources: U.S. Department of Commerce; The Conference Board.

gional detail for its aggregate statistics; regional disparities in the total rate are common. Nevertheless, major movements in the aggregate industry, usually reflecting broad changes in economic conditions and the supply and price of mortgage credit, are generally reflected across the nation.

The housing market takes much of its striking volatility from its dependence on mortgage credit and from the fluctuations, sometimes mountainous, in the interest rates available to mortgage borrowers. When money gets tight (for a description of this condition, see chapter 5 on economic policy), interest rates rise and potential buyers face increasingly unattractive carrying charges. The behavior of the housing market, as measured by the starts rate, is thus a kind of delayed mirror image of the behavior of mortgage interest rates.

Some of the reasons for violent oscillations in the housing market in the past appear to be on their way to removal; builders in the housing industry are now larger, on average, and better established and financed. Deregulation has freed the thrift institutions (those that have survived the savings-and-loan debacle of recent years) that provide much of the mortgage money to compete for funds in the general capital market. The usury limitations on interest rates have been very largely removed, so that the scarcity of funds directly attributable to unworkable legal limitations on mortgage interest rates has almost disappeared. The fact remains, however: Very high interest rates inevitably discourage home buyers and depress the rate of housing starts, while falling rates encourage the markets for both new and existing homes.

While the housing industry is in itself a small component of aggregate economic conditions, its influence on the total can be quite considerable. Falling interest rates stimulate mortgage financing, as well as home purchase; and the creation of a mortgage, either to buy a new home or to refinance an existing home, represents a flow of cash to consumers (this is obvious enough for a refinancing of an existing home, but it is also true for the purchase of a new home, since the buyer generally takes out a bigger mortgage than he is extinguishing on his prior dwelling). For this reason, falling interest rates and a strong housing market tend to enlarge the liquidity of the personal sector and encourage outlay for household goods, other goods, educational outlay, and even vacations. A strong housing market is thus one of the ways in which easy monetary policy and falling rates stimulate the entire system.

A further major longer-term influence on the housing market is the demographic trend, as it appears in periodic projections by the Bureau of Labor Statistics. The present and prospective shape of the U.S. population, particularly by age group, is treated in chapter 8, which deals with the outlook for the longer term. Suffice it here to point out the demographic data look toward a major subsidence of household formation—implying levels of housing starts generally no higher than recent experience and dramatically lower than the experience of the early postwar decades.

Capital Spending and Its Sources

New investment by the private sector is widely considered to be a crucial component of the system's aggregate demand; private investment is the source of future growth and future increases in efficiency, on which improving living standards ultimately rest. **Capital outlay by business** constitutes, on average, about thirteen percent of total demand, but its importance in the business cycle is far greater than the percentage would indicate. Spending by business for investment goods is the classical case of the economist's multiplier effect: A dollar of wages generated in the capital goods industry will go to market in search of a consumer good, which will contribute to the production of another consumer good; wages paid in the course of the production of the second consumer good will seek a third, and so on. (The process attenuates because, at each stage, a portion of the generated income is saved rather than spent.) It is generally estimated that a dollar of output in the machinery industries is worth about three dollars of total GDP. The calculation may be a little loose, but the principle is sound enough. In its ascending phase, investment in plant and equipment is very stimulative to the total system; in its declining phase, it is very constrictive.

Given its importance, it is hardly surprising that the rate of capital spending is the subject of a large data industry, all by itself. In the national accounts, the industry is represented by nonresidential fixed investment, subdivided in turn into nonresidential construction and producers' durables—plain old machinery and equipment (including automobiles bought by the business sector). The U.S. Department of Commerce also produces a quarterly series on business expenditures for plant and equipment, which includes a past record, as well as a measure of anticipated outlays running two calendar quarters into the future. These are the basic data on expected plant and equipment outlay; they play a large role, for obvious reasons, in economic forecasting (see figure 3–4).

The business expenditures series differs from the all-inclusive series in the national accounts in that it excludes agricultural investment, as well as those smaller outlays (such as hand tools) that are normally expensed rather than depreciated. It provides running detail and six-month projections for manufacturing industries and also for mining and service industries, including a broad category of commercial construction.

Behind this basic quarterly series lies a wealth of monthly data on the industry. Activity in the nonresidential construction industry, an important

Figure 3–4. The Trend of Capital Outlay

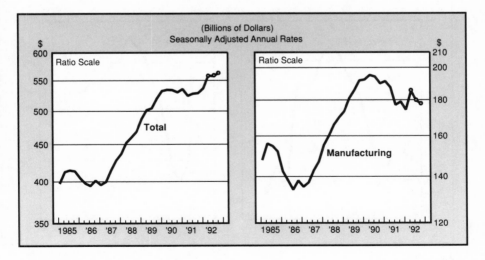

°Anticipated.
Sources: U.S. Department of Commerce; The Conference Board.

part of capital investment, is available monthly, about three weeks after the end of the month, from the U.S. Department of Commerce. It is broken down into a large number of categories: office buildings, industrial structures, shopping centers, and so on. Activity on the machinery side of capital outlay is described in the detailed breakdown of the industrial production index and in the general data on manufacturing industries (discussed below). The machine tool industry, a small but volatile and significant part of the total, is reported on monthly by the National Machine Tool Builders Association.

The Federal Reserve bravely attempts to estimate the **usage rate of capacity** in the U.S. system—bravely, because not much is known about abandonment rates, technological changes in the production functions of individual industries, or changing industry practices with respect to number of shifts. Nevertheless, it is widely assumed that these utilization figures, released by the Federal Reserve on the same day it releases its industrial production index (see below), have substantial bearing on the future of capital outlay (see figure 3–5). It does not take an economist to realize that business will spend very little on incremental plant and equipment at times when it is using only a low percentage of its existing capacity, and that its interest in capital outlay will rise as its current operating rates rise. It is generally assumed that operating rates around eighty-five percent of capacity would be

Figure 3–5. Two Determinants of Capital Outlay

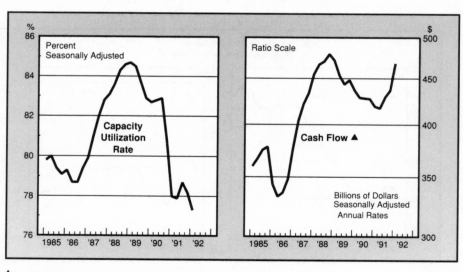

▲Profits after tax plus charged depreciation (including over-depreciation).
Sources: Federal Reserve; U.S. Department of Commerce; The Conference Board.

associated with strong incentives to expand and that these incentives are not present at seventy-five percent of capacity. Of course, about half of all capital outlay is for modernization rather than for expansion (the distinction is powerfully difficult to draw in practice), so capital outlay goes on at all times— very vigorously, indeed, in situations where a new technology is displacing an older, more costly process.

The bulk of capital outlay is performed by corporations. The **corporate cash flow,** which constitutes a major source of funds for capital spending, is thus a further relevant element in appraising the outlook for capital outlay. These figures are generated quarterly, within the national accounts, by adding retained earnings to the U.S. Department of Commerce's measure of corporate depreciation allowances. In the early 1980s, tax-deductible depreciation costs (which constitute a cash flow to the corporation) rose sharply because of the accelerated-depreciation legislation of 1981. The rise in capital spending in 1983 and 1984 was accompanied by (and partly financed by) a surge in total cash flow (figure 3–5). Starting in 1987 (and even partly retroactively into 1986), tax reform has curtailed depreciation and dampened the rise in cash flow. In addition, rising interest payments on corporate debt acted to suppress cash flow. In early 1992, cash flow was actually no higher than it was four years earlier.

Outlays for plant and equipment require financing, of course. A source of the funds, and a principal motive for the outlay, is the cash flow earned in operations. But a strong desire to invest can also be reflected in, and financed by, recourse to "external sources"—the bond market, the equity market, and the mortgage market. In 1991, securities and mortgages accounted for about twenty percent of all sources of funds for nonfinancial corporations. All these data are reported quarterly (but with a considerable time lag) by the Federal Reserve.

Accounting for Corporate Profits

The flow of corporate profits before taxes accounts for only about six percent of all the income flows in the system; it is only about one-fifteenth the size of the personal income flow that goes to individuals. Nevertheless, it is obviously of critical importance as a measure of the conditions prevailing in the corporate sector, under which about eighty-five percent of U.S. business is organized. The rate of corporate earnings is highly sensitive to general economic conditions; relatively small changes in the aggregate GDP can mean large percentage changes in the profits flow.

As described briefly in chapter 2, the national accounts incorporate several measures of profits, of which the most basic is simply **profits before taxes.** The accounts also measure the corporate profits tax burden (on an accrual, not a cash, basis) and profits after taxes. The accounts also make two adjustments to profits accounting, to adjust ordinary corporate accounting to the national income purified concept. All capital gains and losses are removed; profit and loss on inventory is a capital item and is also removed through the famous *inventory valuation adjustment* or IVA, that converts inventory accounting from a first-in-first-out basis to a LIFO basis. (At times of rapid price inflation, inventory profit, which is partly illusory, can become a very large component of profits, as reported in ordinary tax-based statements for corporations). In addition, the U.S. Department of Commerce provides another adjustment for excessive or inadequate tax-based depreciation—that is, the excess or shortfall of tax-based depreciation from what the U.S. Department of Commerce calculates as the true exhaustion of capital. If the inventory adjustment and the depreciation adjustment are subtracted from profits before taxes, the result is an aggregate known as *profits from current production,* which can be thought of as the basic, purified measure of how corporations are doing. If the taxes are removed from this figure, the result is known as **economic profit,** again a basic measure of corporate profitability after taxes (see figure 3–6).

The behavior of corporate profits is very closely correlated with the behavior of the major cyclical components of the system—consumer durables markets (including automobiles), housing, capital spending, and inventory demand. Figure 3–7 shows this relationship and indicates how closely prof-

Figure 3–6. Measures of Corporate Profits

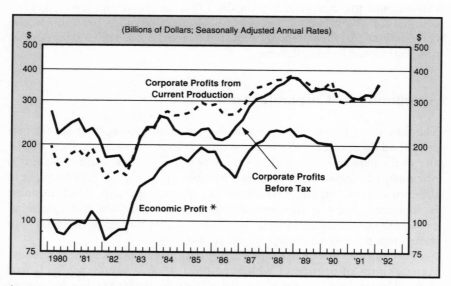

*Profits from current production less tax.
Sources: U.S. Department of Commerce; The Conference Board.

Figure 3–7. The Profits Reaction to the Business Cycle

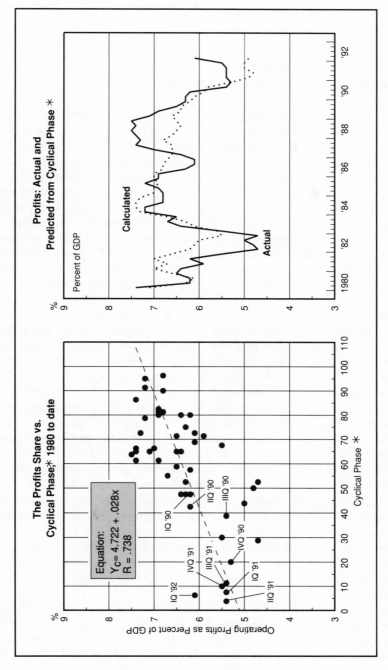

*Measures relative importance of cyclical demands (consumer durables, housing, plant and equipment, and inventory) in total domestic demand.

Sources: U.S. Department of Commerce; The Conference Board.

its can ordinarily be estimated from the behavior of this cyclical heart of the business system.

The Manufacturing Industries:
Production, Sales, Inventories, Orders

The manufacturing sector of the U.S. economy constitutes only about twenty percent of the total, measured in terms of employment. However, although its share in the total has subsided and the share of services has grown, manufacturing activity remains, in many respects, the center of the system—a place where real wealth, as defined by anybody, is created. (There are large differences among economists as to what constitutes wealth creation.) Moreover, manufacturing, being a goods industry capable of experiencing fluctuations in desired levels of inventory holdings, has a special place in the business cycle. (There are, of course, no inventories of services output; services are consumed in the moment of their creation.) And because manufactured goods enter into international trade, the experience of manufacturing industries is heavily influenced by conditions affecting exports and imports.

Around the middle of each month, the Federal Reserve releases its monthly **industrial production index** for the preceding month. The index, among the most watched of all business statistics, measures industrial output (manufacturing, mining, and utilities) for the preceding month, calculating it as a percentage change from the base year of the series, which has recently been revised from an anachronistic 1977 to a less anachronistic 1987. In the industrial production index, a mark of 130 for a month signifies that output in that month, annualized, was thirty percent higher than in the base year. The month-to-month changes in the industrial production index are widely treated as representing the course of general industrial activity in the United States. Since the volatile, cyclical heavy-goods industries carry a disproportionate weight in the index, its behavior is more volatile than that of aggregate output. In general, a six percent annual growth rate of industrial output would suggest perhaps a three percent growth rate in *total* output (see figure 3–8).

The index is available in excruciating detail, all the way down to extremely small subindustries; it is, therefore, a source of close examination, not just by economists, but by sales and planning officers throughout industry as well.

The industrial production index is a measure of physical volume of output. Two weeks after this index appears, the U.S. Department of Commerce issues an immense broadside of data on the dollar value of activity in manufacturing, including **sales, new orders, inventory holdings, and unfilled orders** (backlogs). The release itself carries substatistics for about twenty

Figure 3–8. Real Growth Rates

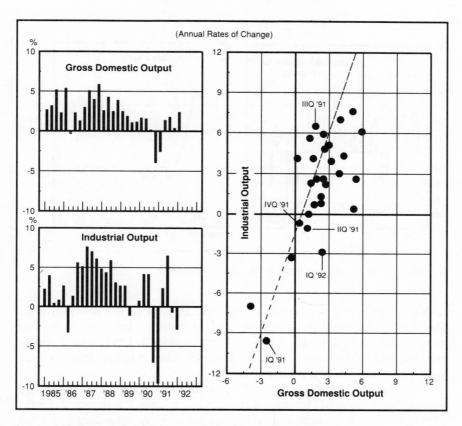

Sources: U.S. Department of Commerce; Federal Reserve; The Conference Board.

major manufacturing industries—all seasonally adjusted but with no adjustment for inflation. These are straight dollar figures, carrying all the significance and limitations that go with value figures. From the figures themselves, it is impossible to say how much of the change from a prior month results from price change and how much from increased physical volume.

Within this immense structure of monthly data on manufacturing, particular interest attaches to the series on new orders, which presumably forecasts manufacturing activity in the future. The series on backlogs, or unfilled orders, helps to describe the direction of pressure on manufacturing activity (rising backlogs would seem to forecast higher production and vice versa) and, most particularly, on the inventory condition of manufacturing.

Inventory conditions play a crucial role in the business cycle (see figure 3–9). Rapidly rising inventories must, in time, suggest that supply has

Figure 3–9. Two Ways of Looking at Inventories

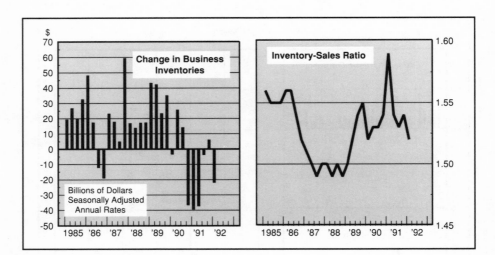

Sources: U.S. Department of Commerce; The Conference Board.

achieved dominance over demand and that, at some future point, production activity will begin to slow. Conversely, rapid liquidation of inventories (as occurred in the last half of 1982 and less rapidly in 1991) would appear to be unsustainable; the very effort to arrest liquidation of inventories would require rising orders and production.

The inventory figures produced within this amalgam of manufacturing data are supplemented about ten days later in a release that incorporates the inventories of wholesalers and retailers, producing an inventory figure for **total manufacturing and trade.** This series covers about seventy percent of all inventories in the system (excluded are agricultural inventories, inventories held by the construction industry, and inventories of nonmerchant wholesalers—wholesalers who do not take title).

This inventory concept differs from the inventory figures encountered in the national accounts, both because of these exclusions and because they are not corrected for whatever price appreciation (or depreciation) may have occurred in the existing stock of inventory. Since most of the manufacturing world is still on FIFO accounting, rising prices tend to increase the value of inventory, even if there is no actual physical change. The manufacturing and trade inventory data do not correct for this discomfort; in other, now familiar words, no inventory valuation adjustment (IVA) is applied. (The change in business inventories that appears as part of output in the national accounts can be maintained as a running total of inventory holdings. The resulting figure runs higher than the figure shown here for manufacturing and trade inventory, by reason of the difference in coverage. The national accounts figure is broader, but it is only available quarterly and, for that and other reasons, it is seldom used.)

Apart from this inescapable complexity, the aggregate inventory release (which lags about six weeks behind the fact) is an important monthly event for economists and the press. In late 1982, the release disclosed an enormous and unsustainable rate of inventory liquidation and turned the outlook sharply upward. The figures showed immense inventory growth into the first three quarters of 1984, but sales had risen so sharply as to suggest that the expansion of inventory was entirely voluntary and no cause for alarm. This way of looking at inventory—as a ratio of inventory to the sales volume it must support or, briefly, the **inventory-sales ratio**—offers a very useful second appraisal of the figures themselves and is widely used in inventory analysis.

Recently—in the late 1980s and continuing into the 1990s— inventory behavior has grown much less volatile (and therefore, less useful in forecasting). Two reasons for the domestication of this formerly feral statistic are (1) much more efficient management of inventory itself and (2) much less price volatility in the materials industries, reducing anticipatory responses of purchasing agents to price expectations. The inventory data are, nevertheless, an important part of a forecaster's regular diet.

Employment and Unemployment

In the end, jobs, incomes, and living standards are the ultimate criteria of the performance of an economic system. There are many other very important goals for a society as a whole—defense security, quality of life, fairness, personal liberty—but jobs, money, and material living standards are the central measures of pure economic performance. Not surprisingly, the U.S. statistical system generates monthly an enormous volume of information on labor market conditions affecting U.S. workers.

Early every month, the Bureau of Labor Statistics produces the results of a massive sample survey of the employed and the unemployed. The definitions of unemployment make it very nearly a state of mind—that is, without a job and looking for work. The **employment and unemployment** figures, taken together, thus represent the U.S. **labor force,** which has been growing at a rate of about two million a year—but the rate is now falling (see figure 3–10). When employment rises faster than that, as it did most decisively in 1983 and 1984 and again in much of 1987, unemployment shrinks; it is worth noting, however, that it takes job creation at an annual rate even now of perhaps 1.5 million simply to hold the number of unemployed constant. Unemployment is normally expressed as a percentage of the civilian labor force (see figure 3–11). Naturally, the percentage fluctuates dramatically in

Figure 3–10. Population and the Labor Force

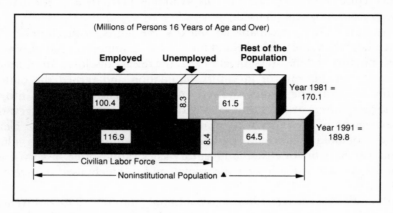

^SExcluding resident Armed Forces.
Sources: U.S. Department of Labor; The Conference Board.

Figure 3–11. The Cycle in the Unemployment Rate

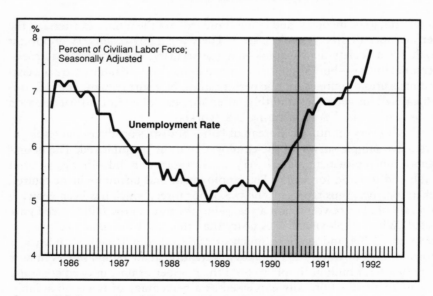

Sources: U.S. Department of Commerce; The Conference Board.

the course of the business cycle; it reached its postwar peak of almost eleven percent at the bottom of the 1982 recession, when almost twelve million Americans were out of work and looking for jobs. (That's deep recession but not depression; at the bottom of the Great Depression in the early 1930s, one in four Americans was out of work.)

Unemployment is a social statistic, as well as an economic statistic. The monthly census offers much material on who is unemployed (by age, sex, race) and the reasons for unemployment (lost a job, left a job, newly entered into the labor force, or reentering the labor force). It is often argued (with some justice) that unemployment compensation tends to elevate unemployment because it permits an unemployed person to look longer for an appropriate job; but that is part of its purpose. In any event, it is worth noting that, on average, more than half the unemployed are unemployed because they lost jobs.

In recent years, about sixty-five percent of the work-eligible population has been either working or looking for work. This figure is called the **labor force participation rate.** The one-third not in the labor force includes housewives, students, those unable to work for reasons of health, and so-called discouraged workers—those who are not looking for work because they believe no jobs are available. In part because of the rapid rise of female participation in the labor force, the percentage of all Americans actually at work rose to a new record in 1987 and reached further new records in 1988 and 1989. Since then, a flattening out of the female participation rate and an actual decline in the male participation rate have slowed the growth of the so-called work ratio and of the labor force itself.

The Census Bureau measures of labor force, employment, and unemployment are reported simultaneously with a measure of nonfarm employment produced by a large sample of actual payroll statistics, yielding figures on what is commonly called **nonagricultural employment.** The figures differ from the census results conceptually, in that they exclude the self-employed and agriculture but pick up the double employment of those working at two jobs. The nonagricultural employment figure is available in considerable industry detail for goods and services industries.

Changes in levels of employment are frequently accompanied by (and often preceded by) changes in the length of the **work week.** This condition reflects the natural incentives of employers, who tend to lengthen the work week in the early stages of recovery before engaging in the costly practice of hiring additional trainees. Conversely, as volume falls off, the work week tends to shrink before employers lay off their existing trained labor. The length of the work week thus becomes a leading indicator of business conditions.

Figures on the length of the work week are published in what is called the "establishment basis" payroll survey. Analysts often multiply the employment figures by the work week figures to get a measure of total labor input into the system each month. Since labor is the predominant ingredient entering into economic activity, the monthly labor input measure is a good indicator of the direction of economic activity.

Prices, Wages, and Productivity

By its nature, economic activity proceeds in an inescapable mixture of physical characteristics and price characteristics. Every transaction in the market is ultimately valued in dollars; its trace in the statistical record reflects neither the physical units nor the price but a compound of the two. Only in the narrowest of individual markets—say, the market for copper, or basic chemicals—is a physical unit of measure readily available. In the common case—for example, measuring the real output of the General Electric Company, or even of the steel industry—a dollar-value aggregate is the commonly available figure.

Changes in prices affect the whole stream of economic activity and stretch a veil—a so-called money illusion— across all the published data on sales, profits, and incomes of companies, industries, the economy as a whole, and, of course, individuals themselves. The statistical system accordingly pays a great deal of attention to price information in order to develop price indexes by which money values can be deflated to represent the underlying realities free from their price influence. The composition of such indexes—*index number construction*—is a highly developed statistical specialty. For our purposes here, the thing to note is that a *price index* combines the prices of many items through a weighting system that reflects the *relative importance* of the items in a *base period* for which a detailed array of expenditure patterns is available.

What is taken to be the major and most general price index for the U.S. economy is derived from the national accounts. The procedure for this deflation is described in chapter 2; the resulting index represents the U.S. price level, and changes in it are considered the general rate of inflation prevailing in the United States. The deflator is, of course, available for the individual components of the output side of the national accounts, yielding real rates of change in all major demand sectors.

Behind this deflator and its various components lies an immense body of price data, organized into indexes that run from daily and weekly (for commodity prices) to substantial monthly indexes of prices for whole sectors of the system. The two principal monthly price indexes are the **consumer price index** (the well-known CPI), which expresses prices at the retail level of goods and service prices, and the **producer price index** (the less famous PPI), which describes trends in the wholesale price level.

The consumer price index is an effort to represent, in one number, the price level (and the rate of inflation) confronting U.S. consumers (see figure

3–12). It covers services as well as goods; its weighting structure represents the composition of outlay of urban consumers (the expenditure survey on which the weighting structure is based was done in 1982–1984). About eighteen percent of the present index relates to food prices and over forty percent to housing, including the costs of renters and homeowners and including fuels, household furnishings, and household operations. The weighting system of the index is a revelation of the importance of ongoing outlay to the consumer; new cars account for only five percent of the weight of the index. Major moves in the index, as in 1974, 1979, and 1987, usually reflect large gains in food, housing costs, or both, but a spreading wave of price movement may well begin in a narrow but crucial sector, such as petroleum products.

Because it represents the price level confronting consumers, the CPI is frequently used to adjust personal incomes, converting them into their real purchasing power equivalents. The index is also widely used in labor negotiations, as an indication of the rate of price increase to which wage earners have been subjected. It is embedded as a measure of the required cost-of-living adjustment (COLA) in union contracts and in social security legislation. In such arrangements, the change in the index calls for an adjustment in an income flow; the income thus is said to be subject to *indexation*.

The release of a new monthly CPI and the calculation of its change from the preceding month always precipitate press comment on the general trend of inflation, not simply because it represents inflation itself, but because it is contractually linked to so many income flows. Extreme rises in the CPI thus have powerful offsetting effects; they deflate the existing income flow (they reduce its real-equivalent purchasing power), while evoking a demand for faster growth of private wages and benefit incomes, contributing to a so-

Figure 3–12. Composition of the Consumer Price Index

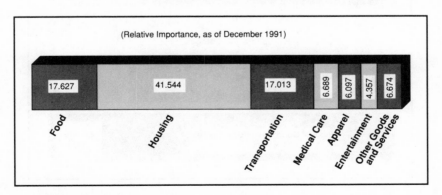

Sources: U.S. Department of Labor; The Conference Board.

called wage-price (or price-wage) spiral. (Inflation is often also attributed to excessive monetary stimulus; see chapters 5 and 7.)

The producer price index measures price developments at the wholesale price level of finished goods, underlying the retail level. Unlike the consumer price index, the PPI is concerned only with goods. The published PPI features finished goods, but the index is a component of a broader wholesale price index, of which other components express price trends in intermediate (semifinished) goods and crude materials for further processing. The aggregate of all three levels is called the **wholesale price index** (WPI). The intermediate index presumably forecasts future prices of finished goods, and the crude materials index forecasts future prices of intermediate goods. The index also provides a number of special groupings, including groupings for capital goods bought by business, and for food, energy, and consumer goods less food and energy. Within the finished goods category, finished consumer goods account for about seventy-five percent of the total weight and capital equipment for about twenty-five percent. Over one-third of the finished goods index is accounted for by food and energy; explosions in these particular categories (as occurred twice for each category in the 1970s) can drive the producer price index to extreme levels not representative of the behavior of the wholesale price level as a whole (see figure 3–13).

Figure 3–13. Composition of the Producer Price Index

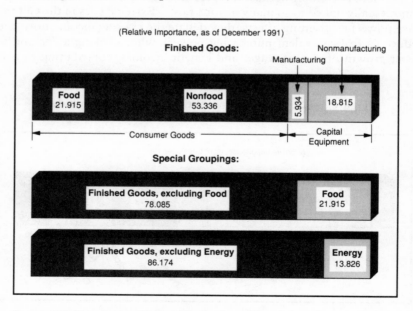

Sources: U.S. Department of Labor; The Conference Board.

In the 1970s, the explosions of food and energy prices drove both the consumer and wholesale price levels up very sharply. These increases were also associated with extremely rapid rises in mortgage interest rates, and the combination led to an extraordinary and partly unrepresentative explosion in the CPI as a whole, which reached close to a twenty percent inflation rate during 1974 and again in 1979–1980. (In times when prices are rising rapidly because of strong demand, the inflation is often called a **"demand-pull"** **inflation,** reflecting excess demand in the system. When the pressure on prices comes from the wage side, it is called a **"cost-push" inflation.** The distinction is not always very clear or usable by policy, since both kinds of pressure are normally present at the same time, and interact in bewildering ways.)

In addition to these price indexes, a multitude of indexes covering traded raw commodities are available from a variety of sources. Individual indexes within this group can behave very differently, depending on the commodities included. The behavior of these **commodity prices** is presumed to reflect world supply conditions, not just U.S. conditions; they are also— and partly for that reason—interpreted to indicate generalized tides of inflation and deflation as they affect the world economy.

The Bureau of Labor Statistics also produces a broad range of data on the earnings of Americans—most particularly, the **average hourly and weekly earnings** of employees in nonagricultural industries (see figure 3–14).

Figure 3–14. The Trend in Earnings, and Their "Real" Equivalents

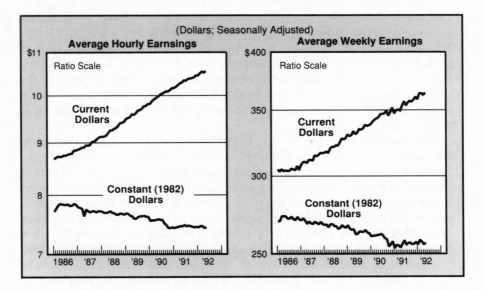

Sources: U.S. Department of Labor; The Conference Board.

The figures are available separately for manufacturing as a whole and for a considerable range of industries within manufacturing. They are also available on a so-called constant-dollar basis—that is, after adjustment for prices—that reveals trends in the real purchasing power of hourly and weekly earnings. Percentage changes in the current-dollar earnings, before adjustment for prices, are taken to be the general rate of wage increases in the United States, as reflected, not in negotiated contracts, but in actual hourly and weekly pay. The Bureau of Labor Statistics also compiles data on wage settlements above a certain size throughout the United States and computes the average size of settlement for the first and ensuing years. But it is the monthly release on wages and their real purchasing power equivalent that makes the news.

Finally, the same energetic Bureau of Labor Statistics brings together a broad range of quarterly data on business output, hours of work, output per hour, compensation per hour, and unit labor costs for the business sector as a whole, for the business sector excluding agriculture, and for manufacturing industries as a whole. These are extremely valuable data, even though they are available only quarterly. Most particularly, the data on output per hour represent the definitive U.S. series on the rate of gain in labor **productivity**—a crucial measure of the efficiency with which labor is being used. Moreover, if compensation per hour is taken together with output per hour, the result is a series of numbers called **unit labor cost,** which in turn is a fundamental measure of the pressures of labor cost on prices (see figure 3–15). Customarily, near the peak of the business cycle, wages are rising rapidly and productivity is declining, resulting in rapid increases in unit labor cost and hence in inflationary pressure on the price level. Early in an ensuing expansion (for example, in 1983), wages rise slowly and productivity rapidly, with the result that unit labor costs are rising slowly or not at all, and upward pressures on prices are minimal. Note from figure 3–15 that labor-cost inflation has subsided persistently in the early 1990s. In general, the trend of unit labor cost revealed by this series is closely related statistically to the behavior of the producer price index; this parallel is often drawn in charts.

Productivity measures have an importance apart from their influence on unit labor costs and prices. If export and import trends are ignored for the moment (but only for the moment: the crucial current significance of export and import trends is taken up in chapter 6), a society can consume only what it produces. Given its labor force, its output—and hence its consumption and its living standards—is determined in the end by the economic efficiency of its labor—that is, its labor productivity. The influences bearing on labor productivity include the size and quality of the capital stock as determined by the rate of business investment in new plant and equipment (which, in turn, is influenced by the profitability of existing investment). They also include the educational level of the labor force and such intangibles as the culturally determined attitude toward work and, of course, the quality of

Figure 3–15. The Structure of Labor Costs

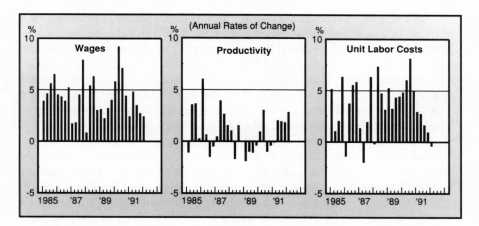

Sources: U.S. Department of Labor; The Conference Board.

management itself. Productivity data thus provide a broad commentary on the efficiency of the entire socioeconomic structure.

Financial Data: The Capital Markets

The United States is absolutely deluged with financial data on a daily basis: The prices on an awesome range of financial assets—stocks, bonds, mutual funds, options, commodity and financial futures, even stock indexes, and even futures contracts on stock indexes—are reported daily and even hourly. This immense flow, occupying a dozen pages or so in every daily newspaper, is the inescapable daily reading of individual and institutional investors. The flow tells what is happening to the values of the enormous range of financial instruments now available to the investor. It represents the broad surface of U.S. financial markets.

Standing underneath this surface and, in many ways, dictating its behavior is the U.S. capital market, in which the price trends of securities are shaped and driven. In real terms, the U.S. capital market is far and away the largest in the world (qualification is not now necessary; the Japanese market, now far past its peak, was for a time much larger when measured in local currencies). Its attractions—its liquidity and efficiency, as well as its enormous size—make it the overwhelming preoccupation of financial investors all over the world. To tap the demand, U.S. financial organizations—banks, investment bankers, brokers—have established themselves in all the other major financial markets (there are more U.S. banks in London than there are British banks). The whole world's financial market now participates globally through electronic data systems. The world has become one huge financial market, and the U.S. market is its major national component.

The stream of information on the U.S. capital market is provided by a number of U.S. economic agencies, but by far the overwhelming share of the data emerges from the Federal Reserve System. The absolutely fundamental published source is the so-called **flow of funds** data system, released quarterly by that agency. Unfortunately, the preparation time is long; the release generally appears several months after the end of the quarter to which it applies. It is, nevertheless, the crucial underpinning of any understanding of the U.S. capital market and the behavior of its participants.

The flow of funds data describe, in the first instance, who has supplied capital to the market and who has drawn it out. Summary statistics are available for each of the major sectors—the household sector, the business sector, the government sector, the rest of the world—and by form of financial instrument—stock issue and purchase, bond issue and purchase, mortgage issue and purchase. Separate tables reveal the activity of the nonfinancial sector, the financial sector, and the aggregate. Taken together, the tables in the flow of funds are a vast sources-and-uses accounting system for the U.S. capital market. Like any such system, the sources conceptually equal the uses, although they are separated by the usual statistical discrepancy.

Drawing on these aggregate flows, the Federal Reserve constructs flows for individual sectors, of which the most significant and most widely used is the structure of accounts for the household sector (see figure 3–16). The tables on households and their behavior provide a far clearer picture of their financial transactions than can be derived from the simple statements of income, spending, and aggregate saving that are provided by the national accounts. Here we get a detailed portrait of personal saving and of the repositories (by kind of financial asset) into which the saving is flowing. The tables also provide detailed measures of the net increases in personal debt—in the form of short-term consumer credit, mortgages, trade debt, and securities debt. The accounts for the corporate sector provide measures of gross investment in physical assets and details of changes in the financial positions of corporations—the changes in their holdings of the whole range of liquid assets in which corporations keep their funds. Comparable tables cover state and local governments and the federal government itself.

The bulk of material appearing in the flow of funds releases deals, naturally, with dollar increases and decreases in the holdings of financial assets. A summary table in each release relates these changes to the underlying stock of debt; that is, it relates increases or reductions in debt to the volume of debt outstanding, for the system as a whole, and for five principal sectors (see figure 3–17). The chart focuses powerfully on what may be the central statistic of the capital market: the **growth rates of debt outstanding.**

To calculate the growth rates of outstanding debt requires a balance-sheet measure of the *level* of debt. Formerly once a year (but now quarterly,

Figure 3–16. Household Assets and Liabilities

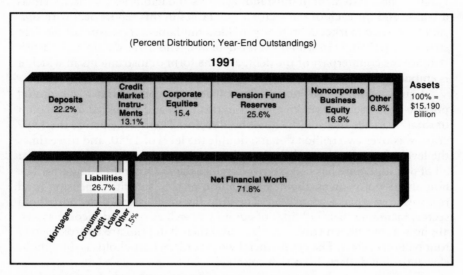

Sources: Federal Reserve; The Conference Board.

Figure 3–17. Growth Rates of Debt Outstanding

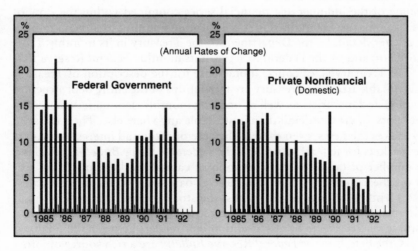

Sources: Federal Reserve; The Conference Board.

with a lag running to about six months), the Federal Reserve produces a balance-sheet statement of **outstanding assets and liabilities** for the system as a whole and for each of the sectors. The tables in this report deal with *outstanding* credit market debt; they provide a fundamental measure of the debt structure, according to who owes the debt and who owns the financial assets that are the counterpart of the debt, and the form of instruments in which it is embodied.

Equity securities are not a form of debt, of course, but a substantial portion of household wealth appears in this form and is carried in the count of total financial assets in the household sector. Their value before the 1987 crash was over two trillion dollars, double the level of 1980, and three times the level of 1975. (As much as $800 billion was lost in the 1987 crash, but all of that and more has been recovered since then). Other useful figures: The household sector owns about $900 billion of U.S. securities; pension fund reserves now equal $3.5 trillion. The total financial assets of the household sector, including their holdings of equities as well as of fixed-income assets, are now about fifteen trillion dollars, and their liabilities are approximately four trillion dollars. The net financial worth of U.S. households is thus about eleven trillion dollars. It's a rich country.

The flow of funds accounting system is integrated with the national accounting system and provides an essential financial background for the flows of output, expenditure, and income provided by the national accounts. As with the national accounts, the volume of detail is immense. The quarterly release receives very little attention from the business press, but an examination of the accounts, as they appear (the release is available directly from the Federal Reserve), always provides additional insights into the behavior of the financial markets.

Some of the innumerable financial series contained within the flow of funds accounts are maintained in more current condition (that is, monthly), or in greater detail, by the Department of the Treasury in its monthly *Treasury Bulletin* and by the Federal Reserve in its monthly *Federal Reserve Bulletin*. The Treasury is, of course, home base for the description of Treasury debt. Available from the Treasury are tabulations of the entire debt structure by coupon and maturity, as well as ongoing monthly data on federal outlay and receipts, in greater detail than is available anywhere else. Their issuance rarely makes the news, even though they are of profound interest to dealers in the markets for federal securities. The *Federal Reserve Bulletin* provides a large number of tables on the condition of **capital markets,** including sections on the condition of the commercial banking system, interest rates, terms of lending at commercial banks, the stock market, and federal fiscal and financing operations. Very few of these figures are released to the press, and still fewer receive any press attention. For readers active in the financial markets, the details in the *Federal Reserve Bulletin* are a rich source of information on the market's behavior.

4

How to Watch the Business Cycle

The long history of the U.S. economy, as well as of all other developed market economies, reveals a persistent tendency toward alternating periods of expansion and contraction that together are called the **business cycle.** In fact, long-term economic history, as it appears in broad indicators of economic behavior, can be broken down into an oscillating *cyclical* component, imposed on a long-term growth *trend,* all confused and made difficult to deal with in the short run because of *irregular,* unsystematic, random movements. A schematic illustration of these three types of movement in isolation, and then combined into the living reality of a typical economic series, is seen in figure 4–1. Figure 4–2 shows the long-term history of expansions and contractions in the economy, as determined by the National Bureau of Economic Research, the unofficial but widely respected custodian of business-cycle statistics for the United States.

There are a number of good reasons why a sensitive, interconnected aggregate, shot through with feedbacks from one part of the system to another, should experience a tide of change in one direction, a reversal, and then a tide of change in the other direction, alternately reaching a "peak" at the end of an expansion and a "trough" at the end of a recession. The tide is familiar enough to virtually all businessmen, who sense it in their own operations as the conditions confronting them to go from strong uptrend, to uncertainty, to strong downtrend, and then on into renewed uncertainty, and improvement. The tide is repetitive—*cyclical.* Each business-cycle experience is unique; it takes its duration, its rates of change, and its shape from always unique combinations of the raw materials on which it works—the position of fiscal and monetary policy, legislative changes, accidents of weather, military and other international conditions, and so on. Although each occurrence is unique, the cyclical experience itself draws on several inherent characteristics of modern economies. The characteristics responsible for the business cycle can be modified somewhat—and offset somewhat—by deliberate government effort; but a modern economy will experience the business

Figure 4–1. The Components of Statistical Movement

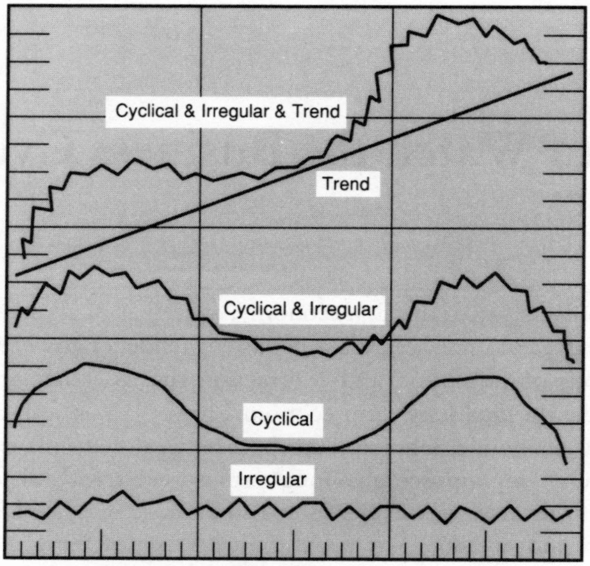

Source: The Conference Board.

cycle in important degree, as long as it retains a predominantly free-market system.

The final expression of demand for all the products and services on the market—the culmination of an economic process in the profitable sale of a good to a willing buyer—draws on a complicated chain of resources and activities that brings the final product in touch with the demand. The supply chain by which an automobile is brought to a dealership for ultimate sale is traceable back through an endless supply chain of fabricated components and then to an enormous range of raw-materials industries—rubber, steel, nonferrous metals, glass, fibers, and so on (see figure 4–3). Changes in the demand for automobiles, as expressed by the sales of dealers, send a demand impulse back along this long and complex chain, giving rise to changes in ordering rates as it goes. Typically, the more complex the product, the more complex the chain. The impact of change at the ultimate point of sale thus sets in motion a *time-consuming* process of adjustment in the same direction. A change in demand, for whatever reasons, is not an event, but an alteration of a rhythm—a shock wave that travels down a long and sensitive line of subdemands within the business system. As the energy is transmitted through these channels, in time it also alters (again, in the same direction) the investment intentions and inventory policies of the industries involved.

The complex supply chains that are characteristic of modern economic

Figure 4-2. Business-Cycle History: Expansions and Contractions

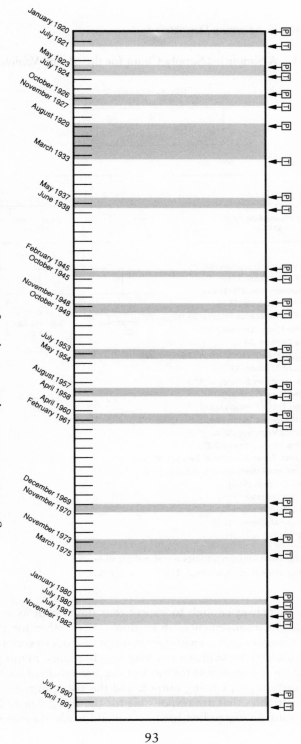

Sources: National Bureau of Economic Research; The Conference Board.

Figure 4–3. A Simplified Supply Chain for the Motor-Vehicle Industry

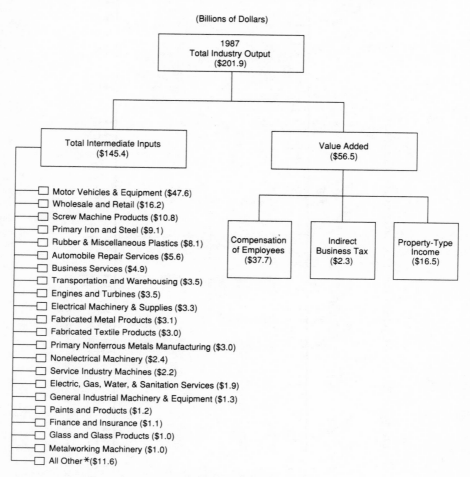

(Billions of Dollars)

*Includes 43 miscellaneous commodities not elsewhere shown.
Sources: U.S. Department of Commerce; The Conference Board.

systems give us reason enough to expect that the system as a whole will engage in sustained movements, up or down, until other forces enter the equation. But another characteristic mechanism of modern societies tends to reinforce the cyclical consequences of long supply chains. In modern economies, production is responsible for most of the generation of income. Rising demand for output yields rising output, and the rising output elevates the very income variables that are responsible for the rising demand. An economy experiencing an expanding level of demand is *always* experiencing an expanding level of income and hence, at least for a time, *further* increment to the demand.

In contrast with the supply-chain effect described here, which operates on only one side of the market, this production-income link can be thought of as a continuous positive feedback leading from more (less) production, to more (less) income, to more (less) demand, to more (less) production.

This process acquires special significance if the change in demand is for plant and equipment and/or inventory—goods that go into the system's balance sheet rather than its operating statement. Higher demand for these *balance-sheet* goods creates income (in the course of their production) that flows into the *operating-statement* markets for consumer goods, creating additional production and, therefore, additional income and, therefore, of course, additional demand. This effect is called a *multiplier;* it means that a dollar of incremental demand for investment goods may yield about three dollars of aggregate increase in the total GDP. And, of course, the multiplier works in a negative direction as well.

Another related mechanism that tends to augment the strength and durability of business cycle movements relates to the presence of very large markets for long-lived durable goods—a distinguishing feature of highly-developed economies. The market for very long-lived goods is characterized by a very low relationship of oncoming supply to the existing stock. For example, refrigerators last, say, ten years, on average. To maintain the existing stock of refrigerators, annual production amounting to only one-tenth of the stock is required. If, for any reason, the market desires a ten percent increase in the stock, the tendency for output is to double—that is, to provide the output required to maintain the existing stock and *then* the output required to elevate it to the new desired level. The longer the good lasts, the lower the percentage relationship of oncoming supply to the existing stock and the more volatile the production response to a change in the desired stock. This *stock-flow* principle explains the extreme amplitude of the production cycle for houses, automobiles, office buildings, and major machinery. (In its application, particularly to machinery, the principle is called the *accelerator.*) This characteristic tends to enlarge the amplitude of the business cycle, though perhaps without altering its timing.

Particularly with respect to investment goods, modern economies experience powerful positive feedbacks from the business cycle in the demand for general goods to a business cycle in the demand for the plant and equipment that produces them—the multiplier and the accelerator at work. As operating rates in general industry rise, margins of available capacity dwindle, and the efforts of individual companies to provide for further growth—and to protect their share of the market—will require them to accelerate the entire cycle by increasing their orders for nonresidential structures and machinery and, probably, for inventory as well.

Thus there are large numbers of plain reasons why a system constructed in the way this one is should experience strong tides of expansion, reinforcing themselves as they go; and then, in reverse, strong tides of contraction that also tend to persevere, to spread, and to grow deeper as they go. Of course, business-cycle expansions do not continue indefinitely, and recessions do not collapse the system down to zero economic activity. The question arises: Why do expansions finally reach a climax, during which the business trend suddenly stabilizes and then reverses into recession; and why do recessions lose their energy and finally give way to renewed expansion?

In addition to the machinery within the economic system that extends and intensifies movement in any one direction, there are also limiting and restraining structures that drag increasingly on the business-cycle movement and finally dominate and reverse it. Among the structural reasons for the system to act in this retardant way, is the simple proposition that increments to the available supply of anything must finally experience declining utility. In the course of a business expansion, the eleventh unit of addition to the stock of consumer goods has a lower utility than the tenth unit; as personal spending continues to rise during an expansion, the *marginal* value of further *spending* declines, while the *marginal* value of *saving* rises. The *marginal propensity to spend* thus declines in the course of a business expansion, whereas the *marginal propensity to save* rises, and an increasing share of personal income finds its way into financial assets rather than the real assets represented in the final demand of consumers, as measured in the GDP. The tendency for spending to lose its energy and for saving to grow is often intensified in the late stages of the business cycle by higher interest rates, which restrict the incentive to borrow in order to spend, and enhance the reward for saving.

The accounts of the federal government also tend to constrain the energy of the business cycle and gradually to arrest its movement. In the course of a business expansion, government revenues used to rise more rapidly than *GDP* itself because of the presence of the progressive personal tax structure. (The indexation of tax brackets effective in 1985 has partly, but not entirely, removed this effect; it remains, in reduced form, in the rise of tax receipts from newly employed workers, in the typical response of corporate profits and the tax receipts from them, and the effects of cyclical inflation on both personal and corporate incomes.) At the same time, government expenditures, which are budgeted in dollars, are not importantly influenced by the business cycle. (Certain forms of social outlay, such as unemployment compensation, are even likely to decline as employment conditions improve.)

The net position of the federal government in the course of a business expansion thus ordinarily moves from the deficit typically experienced during recession toward balance, and the stimulus provided by the deficit in the government account thus shrinks. Conversely, in the course of a recession, the government's income falls, whereas its expenditures are largely unchanged (often, in fact, they increase as a result of efforts to offset recession). The federal deficit tends to widen as activity in the system subsides.

The net budget position of the federal government is thus a countervailing, anticyclical influence on the behavior of the system as a whole, even in the absence of any consciously contracyclical behavior on the part of the government itself. Of course, the contracyclical position of the government is often reinforced deliberately; that is, tax increases almost always occur during expansions and tax reductions during recessions. Monetary policy, too, tends to tighten (thereby inducing rises in interest rates) during expansions and to relax (thereby producing more abundant supplies of credit and lower interest rates) during recessions. (See chapter 5 for a more detailed discussion of the role of economic policy.)

Finally, inventory conditions often provide the climactic event that reverses the business cycle from an expansion phase to a contraction phase and vice versa. As final demands grow more slowly in the late stage of an expansion (remember the diminishing utility of increments to output), inventories tend to grow at the same time that higher interest rates increase the cost of carrying the inventory. Inventory accumulation finally becomes unintended, then reluctant, and lastly, flatly involuntary and undesired. The effort to slow inventory growth, however, means reducing orders to suppliers, who reduce *their* orders to their suppliers, and so on down the long chain of supply described earlier. The effort to curtail inventory is often the crucial reverser of the business cycle into recession; conversely, the effort to reverse an undesired decline in inventory, when final demand stops falling, often converts recession into renewed expansion.

The Cycle in the Statistics

The business cycle is a broad, all-encompassing tide within the business system. Although its focus is in goods industries (in part because that is where the inventory mechanism is at work) few industries—and, therefore, few statistical series—escape it entirely. Its more apparent statistical influences are described here; but practically any industry association and, for that matter, any individual company will find the cycle embedded, in varying degrees of intensity, in its own statistical record.

Because it is such a broad and pervasive phenomenon, the cycle is plainly visible in the record of the national accounts themselves. Figure 4–4 shows the behavior of various components of expenditure and income, as measured in the GDP, in the course of several business cycles (the shaded areas in the charts represent the periods of recession and the unshaded areas the periods of expansion). It is apparent from the chart that considerable parts of the GDP do not seem to experience the business cycle in any significant degree; government demand ordinarily grows in recession and expansion alike, and personal outlays for services appear to operate largely independently of the general business conditions imposed by the cycle.

On the other hand, some components of the GDP react very clearly—

Figure 4–4. Cyclical Behavior in the National Accounts

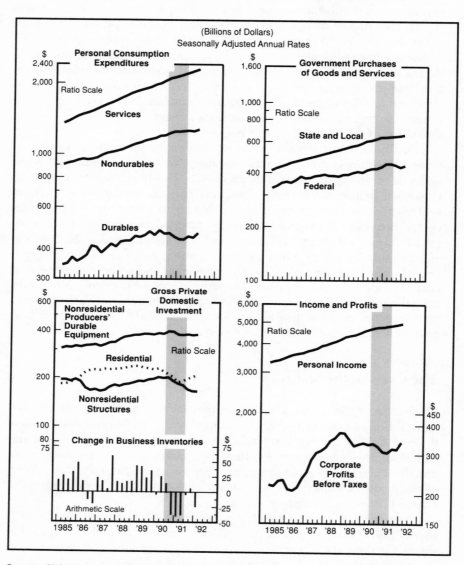

Sources: U.S. Department of Commerce; The Conference Board.

and some of them explosively—to changes in the cyclical phase of the system. These highly susceptible components are, in general, those components where credit formation plays an important part in total demand; and those components, mainly of an investment nature, that involve long-lived durable goods—those for which purchases can be deferred during times of uncertainty, followed by a catching up of demand in times of prosperity (activating the stock-flow principle described earlier). These susceptible components are consumer durables outlays (long-lived and heavily dependent on installment credit); the outlays of business for plant and equipment (also long-lived and credit-dependent); residential building (again, long-lived and credit-dependent); and changes in business inventories (not long-lived, of course, but highly sensitive to the expectations of business with respect to future business volume and prices, and very sensitive to interest rate developments, because the carrying cost of inventory is largely a function of the prevailing short-term interest rate).

Since the sensitivity of the various parts of the GDP to business-cycle conditions differs so much among the components, the internal composition of the GDP changes with the stages of the business cycle. In fact, the internal composition moves in very much the same rhythm as the business cycle itself. Figure 4–5 adds together those parts of the GDP that are most responsive to the cycle and expresses this subtotal as a percentage of total GDP. At the bottom of a recession, the share of the total GDP taken by these sensitive markets is predictably low; it rises in the course of the expansion, reaches a peak just prior to the onset of recession, and then subsides again to its next recessionary trough.

This compositional view of the GDP carries a high information content for forecasting because it describes whether the structure of the system is already very far advanced into expansion and increasingly sensitive to recession or whether it is compressed into the typical defensive position of re-

Figure 4–5. The Cyclical Share of Output

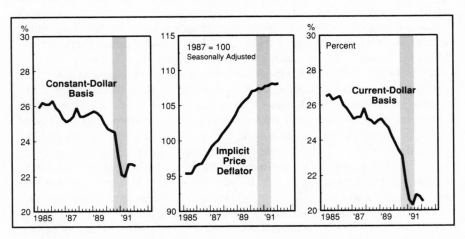

Note: Cyclical share consists of Gross Private Domestic Investment and Durables PCE as percent of Gross Domestic Product.
Sources: U.S. Department of Commerce; The Conference Board.

cession and prepared to respond vigorously to the early stages of a new expansion.

The national accounts components are highly aggregated; they deal only with matters of final sale, and the bulk of them are available only quarterly. For that reason, their value in analyzing the business cycle is limited, and they need to be supplemented by more sensitive indicators, often dealing with orders, production, spending intentions, commitments to future activities—cyclically sensitive data that are available on a monthly basis. Many such useful data have been described in preceding sections; here, some of them are brought together in the context of the business cycle.

One standard approach to appraising the phase of the business cycle is to study individual indicators whose past behavior suggests a stable relationship to the business cycle as a whole. Research by the National Bureau of Economic Research and others has identified a large number of readily available economic series that tend to *lead* the general business cycle; that is, they reach their peaks and troughs before general business and, thereby, at least provide an alert to the probability of a change in the direction of the cycle. Other indicators found in the same search have a record of coinciding very closely with the business cycle itself, and still others exhibit a characteristic *lag;* that is, they reach their peaks and troughs *after* the general business cycle. The three sets of series are called **leading, coincident, and lagging indicators.** In an idealized experience with them, the leading series would pass through a turning point, followed by the coincident series, and then—in a final confirmatory signal—by the lagging series.

The behavior of some of these series over past cycles is shown in figure 4–6. It does not take a very practiced statistical eye to detect a difficulty with this useful but simple forecasting instrument. The series that lead the general business cycle are, in general, much more erratic in their month-to-month behavior than are the coincident, or lagging series, and it is, therefore, much harder to establish a high probability that they are indicating a turning point in the business cycle. Any businessperson will recognize that a series expressing new orders will be much more volatile than one expressing actual ongoing production. Even allowing for the talents of modern computers, the difficulty is inescapable: The series with the longest (and, therefore, most valuable) leads behave most problematically. There are not that many of them, in any event; the business cycle is so pervasive a phenomenon that the great bulk of the available monthly statistical series reach their turning points at very nearly the same time. Nevertheless, the indicator approach to observing the business cycle has distinct value, and the series are watched even by forecasters who also pay a great deal of attention to other devices.

A second approach to observing the business cycle is to focus not so much on how rapidly business conditions are improving or deteriorating, but on how *widespread* the rises or declines in statistical series may be—not on the rate of change of aggregate business, but on the *dispersion* of trends

Figure 4–6. Indicators of Business-Cycle Behavior

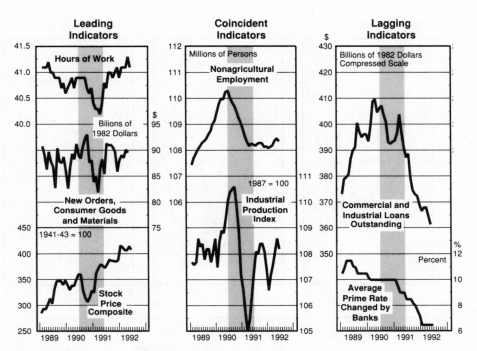

Note: All series seasonally adjusted, except for stock price composite.
Sources: Federal Reserve; U.S. Department of Commerce; U.S. Department of Labor; Standard and Poor's Corporation, Inc.; The Conference Board.

within the aggregate. When aggregate business activity is rising, one would expect that a majority of a reasonably representative collection of indicators would also be rising; when the aggregate system is declining, one would expect that more than half of such a representative collection would be falling; and when total business activity is moving sideways (a rare occurrence, rarely sustained for any length of time), one would expect that about the same number of activities are declining as are rising. This approach studies the dispersion of activity among large numbers of indicators, or their *diffusion*. (A business parallel would be the behavior of a large conglomerate with many more or less unrelated divisions; in an expanding economy, more than half the divisions would be doing very well, whereas in a declining economy, more than half of them would be expected to be doing poorly.)

A number of agencies attempt to capture this sense of dispersion or diffusion in the system by measuring the disparity, in a large number of statistical series, between the number rising and the number falling. The Conference Board's **diffusion index,** shown in figure 4–7, is one such effort. It is

Figure 4–7. The Behavior of the Diffusion Index

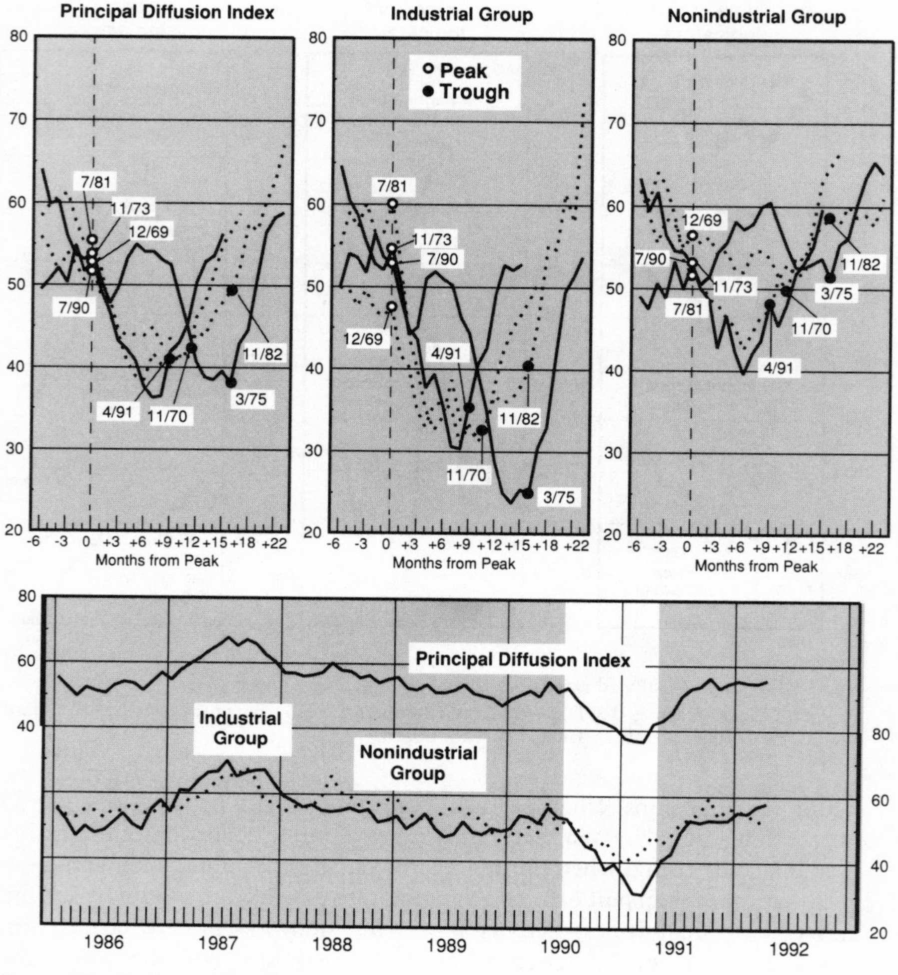

Source: The Conference Board.

composed of twenty series, some of them measuring industrial activities and some measuring trade activities. The principal index measures the percentage of the total series that appear to be rising. The U.S. Department of Commerce's monthly **leading indicator composite,** released about four weeks after the month to which it applies, is similarly constructed and receives enormous (probably excessive) attention from the press. Like the approach through individual indicators, such a device is far from foolproof; yet it does carry information about the width of activities experiencing positive and negative business-cycle trends and has carried imprecise but useful leading characteristics.

Foreshadowing Statistics

By their nature, a number of statistical series *foreshadow* future business activity and are, therefore, useful measures of cyclical tendency. New orders in manufacturing industries forecast the production to satisfy the orders; construction contract awards forecast the construction activity in fulfillment of a contract; new incorporations foreshadow the acquisition of basic equipment by new enterprises. The federal budget itself is a foreshadowing statistic, since there flows from it a stream of budgetary authorizations, appropriations, and obligations that amount to new orders for the goods and services purchased by government. Several of the series referred to as *leading indicators* carry these characteristics.

Foreshadowing statistics have a contractual character, in that foregoing the implied activity carries a cost (the cost of escaping from the contract). Their connection to the business cycle is *causal*, not just statistical. Upstream from these more or less committed orders and contracts are *expectations* series—in general, surveys of *anticipated* outlay, whose findings are not necessarily restricted to contractual obligations.

Consumers are now heavily surveyed with respect to their attitudes, their satisfaction with their financial condition, their personal expectations for the future, and even their buying plans for individual consumer products. Businessmen are surveyed, by the U.S. Department of Commerce and others, for their expected rate of outlay on **plant and equipment** as much as six months to a year ahead, without regard to the proportion of the plans already embedded in firm orders to contractors and machinery producers. Such planned purchases and outlays by consumers and businesses are before the fact, and they can be withdrawn from without cost. They are thus much more erratic and less dependable. Nevertheless, they retain considerable utility and are closely observed. Figures 4–8 and 4–9, respectively, indicate the behavior of a typical survey of consumer attitudes in the course of a business cycle, and the behavior of the U.S. Department of Commerce survey of businessmen's anticipated outlays for plant and equipment.

Other Indicators of the Cycle

The business cycle, as noted, makes its appearance most powerfully among a selected group of markets—those markets that are credit-related and that are composed of relatively big-ticket and long-lived goods. These are the same markets whose aggregate behavior, expressed as a share of GDP, de-

Figure 4–8. Two Measures of Consumer Sentiment

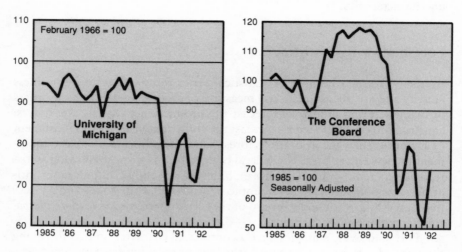

Sources: University of Michigan; The Conference Board.

Figure 4–9. Anticipated Capital Outlays

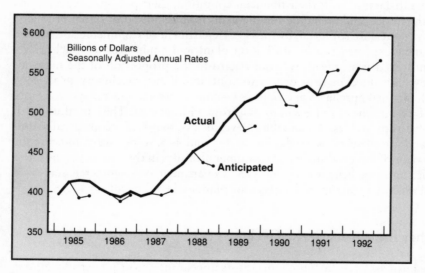

*Anticipated capital outlays.

Note: Extensions of actual plottings are anticipated outlays as of mid-year.

Sources: U.S. Department of Commerce; The Conference Board.

scribes the stage of the cycle in terms of the composition of output. This aggregate behavior of components of the national accounts appears in figure 4–4, but there is a large number of *monthly* statistics bearing on these markets that add important short-term information on the development of the cycle. Some of these series appear in figure 4–10. They include sales rates for automobiles and major household goods, construction starts of residential buildings, machinery ordering rates, and the ongoing monthly change in business inventories. Each of these series is a sensitive monthly reflection of an ongoing investment activity, generally involving extension of credit, and hence reflecting the degree of confidence in the future of buyers (both businesses and consumers). The changes in direction of these series mark important points in the progress of the business cycle simply as a matter of rising and falling fundamental demands, but they also reflect changing attitudes— the flux of collective judgment about the future.

The stock market itself is among the most sensitive and prescient indicators of collective attitudes; in connection with the stock market, it should be noted that major moves in the **values of securities** do not represent simply a forecasting or expectational variable. Important changes in the values of securities have a powerful influence on the balance sheet of the household sector; at present, for example, every point in the Standard & Poor's index is approximately the equivalent of seven billion dollars in personal wealth. The rise and fall of securities prices thus produces a tide of *wealth effects* in the form of realized and unrealized capital gains and losses experienced by the holders. The stock market does not simply *forecast* changes in business conditions; to some degree, it *causes* them, through inflation and deflation of the personal balance sheet and, hence, of the attitudes of the consumer sector as a whole.

Finally, the list of key business cycle statistics includes **interest rates.** Discussion of federal government policies that influence rates appears in chapter 5; here, it is essential to note that fluctuations in rates are powerfully related to the business cycle of the past twenty years. Sharp elevations in interest rates deter buyers and increase the reward for saving; they are thus a major constricting force on business conditions. Conversely, substantial reductions in interest rates lower the cost of credit-oriented purchases and reduce the alternative reward (interest income) for withholding funds from consumption. As figure 4–11 reveals, the general level of interest rates has had a powerful if complex relationship to the aggregate business cycle.

Another set of financial statistics over which economists agonize is the interest rate **yield curve** (see figure 4–12). The yield curve, almost always (but not necessarily) illustrated in the interest rates on Treasury securities, expresses the relationship among rates, at a given point in time, across the spectrum of maturities from short term (three months) to long term (thirty years). When the yield curve is "steep," the reward for investing long-term is large, relative to the yield available on short-term securities; and, conversely,

Figure 4–10. Selected Cyclical Indicators

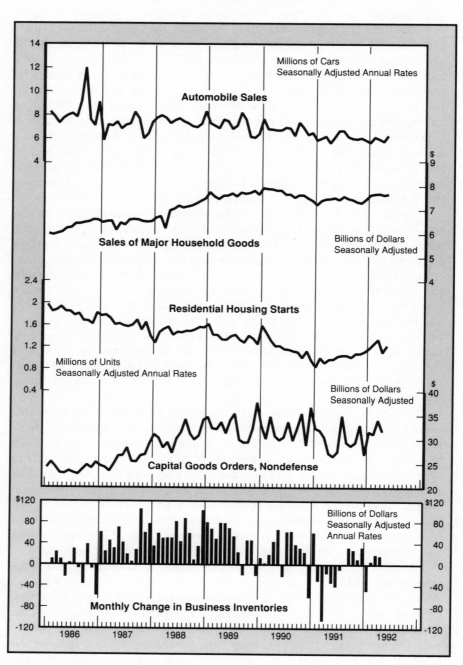

Sources: Ward's Automotive Reports; U.S. Department of Commerce; The Conference Board.

Figure 4–11. The Cycle in Interest Rates

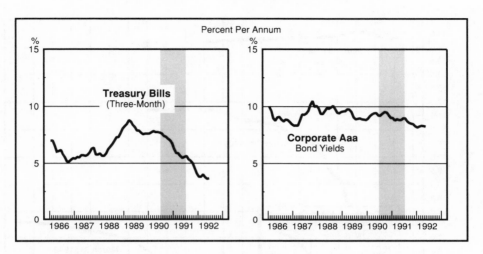

Sources: Department of the Treasury; Moody's Investors Service; The Conference Board.

when the yield curve is flat, the reward for "going long" is modest—even conceivably negative, when the yield curve is said to be "inverted."

The shape of the yield curve reflects several considerations. In the first place, one would think that arbitrage along the yield curve would limit how steep the curve can get; that is, if the reward for going long is very high, investors will be led to avoid the short-term securities (driving down their price and driving up their yield) in order to seek the higher yields available at long-term, thus driving up the demand for long-term securities, strengthening their price, and reducing their yield. But other considerations operate in conjunction with this simple arbitrage across the yield spectrum. If only the arbitrage were at work, the Federal Reserve's efforts to reduce short-term interest rates (which is where the Federal Reserve's power resides) would also produce lower long-term rates. However, long-term investors are hypersensitive to the issue of inflation, since inflation threatens to drive down the value of long-term securities. If the Federal Reserve is aggressive with respect to reducing short-term rates, its very aggressive behavior can stimulate fears of inflation and actually drive long-term interest rates up, arbitrage or no arbitrage. This is a perverse result, since driving up long-term rates certainly hinders growth in the housing market and in the markets for plant and equipment. Any developments that suggest that the Federal Reserve will have to be liberal—for example, to accommodate the huge volumes of federal financing now required to fund the budget deficit—suggest inflationary behavior on the part of the Federal Reserve and act to elevate long-term rates. Finally, the U.S. financial market now rests heavily on inflows on capital from the rest of the world; if these inflows were to be jeop-

Figure 4–12. The Steepness of the Yield Curve

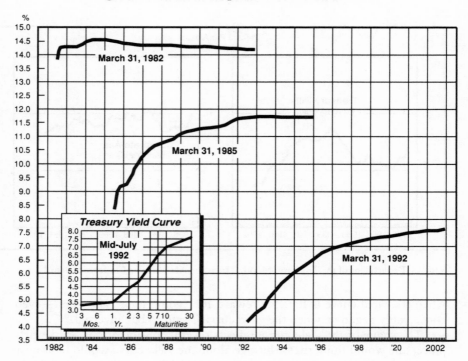

Note: The curves are fitted by eye and based only on the most actively traded issues. Market yields on coupon issues due in less than three months are excluded.

Sources: Department of the Treasury; The Conference Board.

ardized, the whole rate structure, but most particularly the long end of the yield curve, would experience the cautions that drive interest rates up. (Chapter 8, which focuses on the future of the entire system in the 1990s, will make much more of this point.)

A related financial indicator that is highly suggestive with respect to on-coming cyclical conditions is the real value of the money stock—that is, the money stock converted to a measure of purchasing power through "defla-tion" by an index of price trends. The rate of change of this purchasing power measure tends to precede changes in general business conditions (see figure 4–13).

The indicators described in this section make up the regular diet of busi-ness-cycle analysis and forecasting. Each appearance of a new number in these series is searched for its cyclical significance. For long stretches of months, quarters, and even years, these indicators typically throw off signs of continuing growth in economic activity; then they gradually lose their

Figure 4–13. The Cycle in Purchasing Power of Money

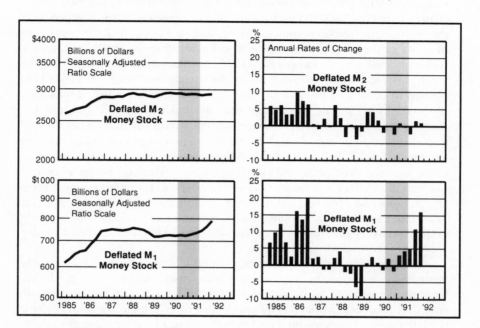

Sources: Federal Reserve; The Conference Board.

coherence as conflicting trends become visible among them; finally—often in a period measured only in weeks—the general impression of cyclical stage conveyed by the numbers changes dramatically, and the consensus of fore-casters, moved by the accumulating evidence, begins to reach toward a fore-cast of recession. As the impression spreads, attitudes throughout the system respond; the response itself enlarges caution and introduces still more pow-erful hesitations into the concerned markets. The climactic moment of the business cycle occurs when a trend reverses and the awareness of the reversal spreads throughout the business, financial, and consumer community—al-tering general expectations, inducing a search for shelter, and inaugurating the pursuit of security and liquidity. Anticipating such a turning point effec-tively, or at least recognizing it promptly, is a necessary and rewarding part of short-term and intermediate-term business planning.

The business-cycle machinery described here is ineradicably present in a free-market system. The cycle subsists in the form of alternating energies—a pendulumlike exchange of potentials from one state (recession) to an ensu-ing reverse state (expansion). Staying with the pendulum simile, it is possible to envision sets of circumstances that would arrest its motion or make it so wobbly and arrhythmic as to give it the appearance of almost random behavior. The environment in which the pendulum operates can be so viscous, so clouded with particular circumstances and criss-cross trends, that the exchange of energy becomes impossible, and the business cycle is stilled, even though the mechanism is intact. This stilling of a cycle, and the suspension of many of the indications of cyclical behavior described in this chapter, is strikingly visible in the experience of U.S. business from the middle of 1984, when a strong cycle recovery from the strong recession of 1981–1982 seemed to come to a halt, all the way into 1990. In late 1987, it was often observed by economic forecasters that the business-cycle expansion had reached a duration of five years (measuring from its beginnings at the bottom of recession in late 1982). The last three years of this period do not look like business-cycle behavior at all; on the contrary, they appear as uncoordinated upward drift, with individual markets (including the great cyclical markets themselves) operating at cross purposes, as though their basic interconnections had been severed. From the fall of 1990 (the onset of the Gulf War) into early 1991, a recognizable recession intervened; thereafter, a brief cyclical recovery gave way to renewed drift until early 1992, when a moderate cyclical recovery began.

In its application to forecasting, economic reasoning and, particularly, business-cycle reasoning, have recently been frustrated. Huge budget deficits have not turned out to be stimulative; the inflation rate, which normally rises during an expansion, has fallen; interest rates, which customarily rise in the late stages of expansion, have fallen dramatically. Abundant availability of credit has fueled explosive behavior in financial markets, while the real world has drifted along equivocally.

There are great and, taken together, quite sufficient explanations for the noncyclical character of business in recent years—a subject pursued into the 1990s in chapter 8. In the first place, the long trajectories of debt, physical holdings of goods, and international competitive position described in chapter 1 have deposited heavy anti-cyclical weights on the system. They have dulled the normal responses of borrowing and investing that are fundamental parts of the business cycle. Second, the fundamental changes in the U.S. position with respect to the rest of the world—most particularly, the fall of the dollar over several years ending in the late 1980s and the incredible surge of imports, partly a reflection of the elevation of the dollar in the early 1980s—have radically altered the position of the manufacturing sector in the system. Manufacturing output, investment, and even inventory policy have been profoundly influenced by the flood of imports from the developed world (Europe and Japan), as well as from a host of newly industrialized countries (South Korea, Taiwan, and Hong Kong, for example). In the presence of these huge tides, one in our domestic history and the other in our place in the world, the wave of the business cycle has been hard to find out there. The amplitude of the cyclical pendulum seems to have been reduced, and its rhythm has been imperfect. Reasons for this dissonant behavior are taken up in detail in chapter 8.

Despite the confusion of the evidence, a revival of the business cycle, in both its expansion and recession phase, remains an expectable development. (It appears to be occurring, but still only hesitantly, in 1992.) The structure of the cycle, as described in this chapter, is unalterably present. It would be a mistake to assume that the force of the cycle, always formidable when it gathers strength, will not reappear in time. The pendulum may now and then seem nearly still, but the machinery is there, to be restarted when conditions again favor a return to traditional volatile patterns of free-market behavior.

5

The Influence of Economic Policy

No businessperson or consumer in the United States (or for that matter, in any developed economy) needs to be told that government, at all its levels, exerts a powerful influence on the behavior of business. Some government policies are specific to individual industries and markets (regulatory policies, antitrust policies); some, such as environmental regulation, accept general economic costs in order to achieve partly noneconomic objectives. Others seek to influence the relationship of the U.S. economy to its trading partners and the rest of the world; still others pursue long-term distributive goals (fair and just distribution of income, elimination of poverty, improved health, job security, higher educational standards) set by ethical considerations as much as by supposed economic benefit. Each of government's multiple objectives, and how well or ill its efforts serve those objectives, is a study in itself not appropriately pursued here (although some strong comment on the current and prospective role of government appears in chapter 8, "The Wave of the Future").

Beyond these specific economic and social goals, however, the government carries a large *general* economic mandate to seek and maintain an economic environment in which *general* economic activity prospers—an environment in which the private sector, composed of private individuals and private corporations, can pursue their own economic interests in a favorable climate of general growth and stability. The mandate and the responsibility are not new: They developed informally and without an explicit legislative base during the Great Depression of the 1930s. The legislative base—the explicit commitment—was put in place in the early postwar years. That legislation, embodied in the Employment Act of 1946, intended to state that henceforth government would use its economic powers to ensure that nothing like the 1930s would occur again. But it has been interpreted, quite reasonably, of course, to mean that government commits itself to the achievement of vigorous growth, a strong job market, and stable prices, all of the time.

In pursuit of this general objective, the federal government possesses two powerful sets of economic instruments broadly characterized as *fiscal policy* and *monetary policy*. The two arms of policy can work together to supplement each other when powerful stimulus or restraint is sought. Or they can work in beneficial or damaging opposition, when one or the other arm is driven off course into excessive stimulation or excessive restraint. The condition of each of the two arms of policy and the relationship between them are among the most powerful forces affecting the course of business in the private sector. Accordingly, the statistics reflecting these conditions are vital and essential guides to the future of business itself.

Fiscal Policy

Fiscal policy means, most generally, the influences on the private sector emanating from the condition of the federal budget—the spending of the federal government, its receipts, its surplus or deficit, and the resultant accumulating debt (see below). Unlike many other sovereign governments and unlike many of the U.S. state governments, the federal government does not engage in capital accounting. Its operations are recorded very nearly as a cash flow—cash income less cash outgo (no balance sheet, no reporting of depreciation of long-lived assets, no net worth or stockholders' equity). When the government buys something, it treats the purchase as a cash outlay, ignoring the asset value of what it bought; when it sells something, it treats the proceeds as income, disregarding the reduction in its holdings of assets.

As this may not be the best way to run a railroad, so it is not necessarily the best way to run a government (there are many sophisticated studies of how the accounting might be improved; see below). But that's the way it is, and that's what the currently available figures mean. A surplus in the federal budget (a very rare occurrence since the 1920s, when a surplus was mandated by law) simply means that the government is experiencing an infusion of cash, which it uses to pay back a portion of its outstanding debt (actually, it means the government is issuing less debt than it is retiring). A deficit (a much more familiar phenomenon, to put it wryly) means the government is experiencing a cash drain, which it finances by issuing additional debt instruments (that is, issuing new debt instruments faster than it is redeeming old instruments). The debt instruments of the federal government are absolutely risk free with respect to the payment of principal and interest (but not necessarily in terms of current value, since the market value of longer-term issues will fluctuate with general interest rates). Being what might be called interest-bearing cash, the increased issuance of government securities enlarges the supply of cash and near-cash in the hands of the private sector and is, therefore, almost without exception, treated by economists as a stimulus to private business and, in extreme conditions, a threat of inflation. The record of all this almost continuous stimulus is shown in figure 5–1, which records the spending, receipts, and deficit or surplus of the federal government and the accumulation of debt instruments by which the debt has been financed, all on a fiscal-year basis (the federal government is now on an October 1–September 30 fiscal year).

The attitudes of economists and even of the population at large have undergone a rather dramatic evolution in the course of postwar history, during which the nation constructed its own American version of a **mixed economy** (see chapter 9 for a more extended discussion of the term). Prior to the depression, which was also prior to the revolution in economics presided over by John Maynard Keynes, a public deficit was sort of sinful; it was widely believed that a government should, like a family, "live within its means." Even Franklin Roosevelt campaigned in 1932 on a platform that included a balanced federal budget. But events and then theory have gradually destroyed this moralistic and impractical view. Keynes argued that the government had an important stabilizing role, particularly since private in-

Figure 5–1. Federal Receipts, Outlays, and Debt

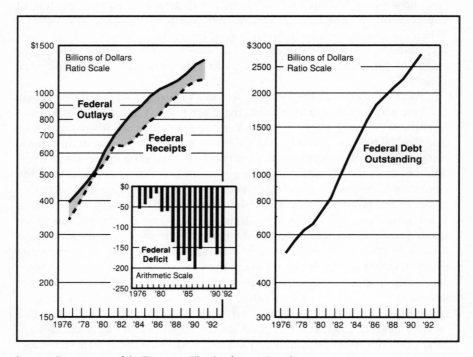

Sources: Department of the Treasury; The Conference Board.

vestment activity was intractably variable and undependable and, therefore, destabilizing and, therefore, required periodic offset when it was weak. This reasoning suggested, in the first instance, that the federal government might run a deficit in bad times and then a surplus in good times, producing stability over the long run and no growth of federal debt outstanding. In the 1960s, this essentially cyclical view of budgeting gradually gave way to the doctrine that the budget should be balanced in good times and run a stimulative deficit in bad times—a view that permitted long-term growth of the public debt outstanding. This is still probably the prevailing view, although it is now held very weakly indeed, since budget deficits have been virtually continuous for decades, in good times and bad times alike, and the growth of the federal debt has been little short of spectacular.

With the virtual abandonment of the absolute moralistic position on how the federal budget should balance itself, it has been very difficult for economists to find an amoral rule to serve as a guide in budgeting. What has emerged in recent years is the argument that the budget deficit should be restrained to such a level that the resulting growth in the federal debt outstanding would be stabilized as a percentage of the GDP; that is, the growth rate of the debt should not exceed the growth rate of the economy as a whole. This rather pragmatic and perhaps logically unsatisfying guide rule has also been observed in the breach for two decades; figure 5–2 reveals how the relationship of the debt to the GDP has grown rather dramatically for

Figure 5–2. Federal Debt and Its Relationship to GDP

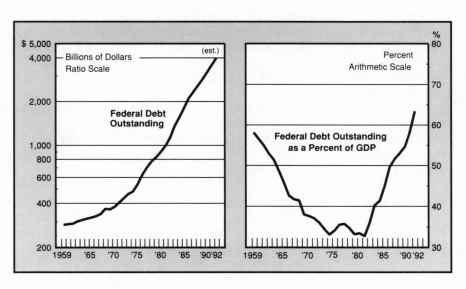

Sources: Department of the Treasury; The Conference Board.

fifteen years. And the absence of any very visible relationship between the growth in the debt, the growth in GDP, and the inflation rate have tended to dilute the support, even for this less onerous rule.

Because deficits are now considered stimulative in any first-round analysis, they are widely accepted as appropriate at times when the economy appears to need stimulus. This is most particularly true, of course, during general recession with its accompanying unemployment. Historically, the big deficits have been experienced precisely during recession, simply because private incomes fall during recessions, and, therefore, the revenues of the federal government decline, whereas budgeted spending is unaffected by recession (the effect of recession on spending is generally to enlarge it through higher unemployment compensation payments and other deliberately stimulative spending efforts). Deficits produced in this way are often called *passive* deficits, or **cyclical deficits,** because they result mainly not from intentional policy moves, but as a reaction to recession itself. In an important sense, such deficits *measure* the severity of the recession and *cushion* the private sector as it declines. This is the point on which Keynesian budget theory focused.

Since nobody particularly likes recession, the deficits experienced in the course of one are often deliberately accentuated by tax reduction (which further suppresses government revenues) or by deliberate *contracyclical* spending programs. Even in the absence of recession, tax reductions (such as those instituted by the Reagan Administration) and/or spending increases can drive the budget into a position where it would run a deficit, even under generally prosperous economic conditions. Such a deficit is called a *secular* or *structural* deficit, or a **cyclically adjusted deficit.** Economists have struggled for decades to achieve separate measures of the *cyclical* and the *structural* deficit—that is, the part of the deficit that simply results from underemployment and recession in the private economy, and the part that reflects the real longer-term position of the deficit attributable to the tax rates imposed by the federal government and its spending—a mismatch of the expectable revenues from the tax structure, on the one hand, and the spending intentions on the other hand. The latest effort at this calculation, which yields a cyclical deficit and a cyclically adjusted deficit (the secular deficit), appears in figure 5–3. (The aggregate recent history of the deficit, as calculated in the national accounts, was discussed in chapter 2.)

The difference between the cyclical deficit and the secular or structural deficit is crucial to appraising the budget position. By definition, the cyclical deficit reflects the presence of idle resources; the stimulus provided by the deficit can be expressed in rising real production activity. A structural deficit, however, already adjusted to high employment conditions, implies stimulus beyond the ability of real production to respond. It is, therefore, a probable cause of inflation in ordinary times. The fact that it did *not* cause inflation in the years since 1984, when deficits have grown to and stayed at

Figure 5–3. The Federal Budget Position

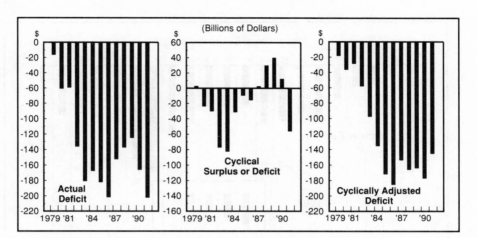

Note: Year 1991 is estimated; series in process of revision.
Sources: U.S. Department of Commerce; The Conference Board.

levels that used to be unimaginable, is an indication of how abnormal the times have been—or, alternatively, how weak theoretical reasoning is with respect to the consequences of budget conditions (see below).

If, like most economists, we accept the proposition that budget deficits are inherently stimulative, then it is well worth looking at their present and prospective position. For a decade, the federal government has been required by law to produce five-year projections of revenues, expenditures, and surpluses or deficits, based on its proposed intentions with respect to taxes and outlays, and on the prospects for the state of the economy. Figure 5–4 discloses the evolution of these five-year forecasts since 1987. The picture was one of projected progress out of deficit and into surplus all the way through the 1986 budget submission; ever since, anticipated deficits rule emphatically in all the five-year projections, still more immoderately in recent years. The conclusion must be that, unless revenue and expenditure trends are to be altered to equal or beat the latest projections, the federal budget will be in a powerfully stimulative, perhaps ultimately inflationary, deficit position far into the 1990s.

Such an unfortunate outcome appeared to be possible as of the fall of 1987. The legislation known as Gramm-Rudman-Hollings (or, for brevity, Gramm-Rudman) expressed the intention of the Congress and of the administration to move the federal budget deficit sharply downward to a condition of absolute neutrality—that is, a zero deficit—by 1991. But the powers to "sequester" funds and programs, ultimately applied as across-the-board re-

Figure 5–4. Five-Year Budget Projections: The Endless Disequilibrium

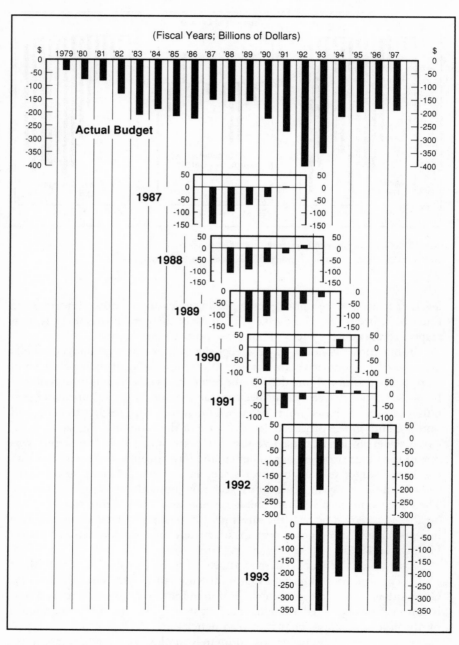

Sources: Office of Management and Budget; The Conference Board.

ductions in spending, ran into constitutional problems. New arrangements for this Draconian way of assuring shrinking deficits are less Draconian but much less dependable. The Congressional Budget Office (a kind of research arm of the Congress on budgetary matters) and the Office of Management and Budget (the wing of the administration charged with the construction and defense of budgets) are often in disagreement with the extent of progress that can be expected and, therefore, the need for still further legislation curtailing the growth of outlay and adding to the income side through tax increases. The projections shown in figure 5–4 for later periods are, therefore, much in doubt. In recent legislation affecting budget conditions, a kind of deal had been struck between a Democratic Congress and a Republican Administration that theoretically required that any increase in spending in any area be accompanied by reductions in other areas or by a tax increase. That too has turned out to be at least partly unworkable.

How did a nation with perhaps the most aggressive orientation toward free markets of any country in the world develop so large a federal budget issue, particularly in the years of Republican administrations? The answer to the paradox lies in the particular objectives of the Reagan Administration, and, to some degree, their frustration by the Congress. The huge budget deficits of the past decade reflected, at first, rapidly rising outlay for defense, on the one hand, and massive reduction in personal tax rates, and hence in receipts of personal taxes, as a consequence of the rate reductions of the years 1982 to 1984. Reaganomics required a degree of curtailment in nondefense outlays that went far beyond the intentions of the Congress. (For the reasons for the resistance to curtailment of such outlays, see chapter 9.) Even at this writing, ten years after the issue of the budget deficit began to assume its present shape and importance, the Congress and the administration are still deeply divided over how much of the deficit gap should be closed by spending restraint and how much through reimposition of taxes.

And a growing minority of economists seems to accept the pragmatic rule that would permit deficits to go on forever. Those who do, seem to suggest that a deficit amounting to say, even $300 billion, should not really bankrupt an economy whose output is over five trillion dollars. On the other hand, a $300 billion use of the country's *savings*, which amount to only about $700 billion, looks much more ominous. Impressed with this latter very relevant statistic, representing a major impairment of the nation's ability to invest, even liberal economists argue that the deficit must be reduced, if the nation is to grow vigorously in the future.

Fiscal Flux

A further extended note on what may fairly be called the "budget crisis" of 1992, incorporating and extending the conventional description of the budget issue above, is necessary.

For fiscal 1992, the federal budget year ending September 30, the present estimate of the deficit is about $449 billion, or 7.7 percent of GDP. In the most common of all adjustments to this gross figure, one might restore the surpluses of the trust funds, now running about fifty billion dollars. The aggregate deficit, including the operations of the trust funds, thus appears to be about $400 billion, a nice round number representing 6.8 percent of the GDP. These figures are, of course, the biggest in history, but they follow upon a long stream of deficits. The on-budget deficit has been $200 billion or higher since fiscal 1983, with the only exceptions of 1984, 1987, and 1988. The accumulating debt representing the financing of these deficits, including that held by the public and by government agencies, is now about four trillion dollars; it has almost tripled since 1983 and doubled since 1986.

These are impressive numbers, readers will agree. Readers may also agree, having listened to anguished discussions of the numbers for years, that nobody knows for sure what they mean; nobody knows whether or not the accounting system that produces them means anything; nobody knows the consequences of a deficit, however measured. Nobody knows for sure how the behavior of the Federal Reserve affects the consequences of any particular deficit; nobody knows the interest-rate implications of the two sets of policies combined; nobody knows the effects of alterations in the composition of the spending and revenues reflected in the deficit numbers. Nobody knows what inflation consequences should be attributed to any given level of the deficit, in absolute terms, or relative to the GDP or the system's private saving rate. Lots of theories: loads of numbers; no agreement; no assured knowledge. The problems confronting economists with respect to the deficit resemble those of physicians practicing medicine prior to Harvey's discovery of the circulation of the blood. The subject itself certainly appears more important at a $450 billion deficit than when the deficit was much smaller, or nearly zero, but the ignorance was really just as great under those conditions.

The budget presents several deep questions, none of which has ever been resolved to the satisfaction of the superior minds of theoretical economists, much less the ordinary minds of the rest of us. A first question is what does the present accounting system mean? A second question is how good is the present accounting system, and what variations on it would produce what results? Third, however calculated, what are the consequences of a budget deficit? And fourth, what difference does it make, if any, as the composition of spending and revenues underlying the budget has changed over time?

What is meant by the term "deficit" used in all of the theoretical arguments? A sophisticated accountant (yes, Virginia. . . .) will agree immediately that any number produced in an accounting statement has two and only two qualities: a dimension and a meaning; the meaning arises out of the accounting conventions and definitions by which it is produced. A budget deficit may be big or small, but its meaning and its interpretation rest upon the accounting system that yields it.

The accounts regularly calculate an on-budget outcome, then an off-budget outcome reflecting the surplus operations of the trust funds, and then a total budget outcome (lines 1, 2, and 3 of table 5–1). *Line 3 comes close to representing the gross cash flow between the federal government sector and the rest of the economy.* While there are certainly peculiarities in this calculation, there are no inscrutable mysteries. Indeed, the cash flow shown on line 3 bears a powerful general resemblance to the term as it is used in ordinary business accounting.

From here on, it's every man for himself. Line 4 deducts from the deficit the dollar volume of debt service to public holders of Treasury securities. The rationale for this deduction is a bewildering mixture of emotion and logic. It rests on the proposition that the debt out there resulted from past budgets, not this one, and that the harried legislators in Washington should not charge the current deficit with the history of past deficits. In any event, the resulting deficit is called the *primary deficit;* weak as it is, it holds some status as a named outcome and enters into debate on the meaning of the deficit.

Table 5–1
Illustrative Manipulations of the Federal Accounts for Fiscal 1992

	Billions of Dollars	Percent of GDP	Percent of Gross Private Saving
1. On-Budget Deficit	$449	7.65%	48.73%
2. Less: Off-Budget Surplus	49	0.83	5.32
3. Equals: Aggregate Deficit	400	6.82	43.41
4. Less: Debt Service	190	3.24	20.62
5. Equals: Primary Deficit	210	3.58	22.79
6. Less: Inflation Tax	85	1.45	9.23
7. Equals: Adjusted Primary Deficit	125	2.13	13.57
8. Less: Cyclical Deficit	60	1.02	6.51
9. Equals: Structural Deficit	65	1.11	7.05
10. Less: Investment in Nondefense Physical Facilities and Grants-in-Aid	55	0.94	5.97
11. Equals: Net Structural Government Consumption	10	0.17	1.09

Sources: Office of Management and Budget; The Sommers Letter.

The next adjustment in table 5–1, also recognized in the literature, argues that the government should be credited with the effects of inflation in reducing the real purchasing power of the outstanding debt. Line 6 in the table represents the lost purchasing power of the outstanding debt held by the public (about three trillion dollars) in the presence of about a three percent rate of inflation. This makes a little (not too much) sense in the same way that the Federal Reserve must pay some attention to the effects of inflation on the purchasing power of the money stock. (In general, inflation favors debtors, as we all know.) But it is really full of paradoxes and misshapen mirrors: Since all the accounts that produce the deficit are in current dollars, it seems a little grotesque to shift to a constant-dollar measure of the outstanding debt. The effect of the adjustment is to place into a particular relationship the debt service of the federal government and the impact of inflation on the holders of the debt. For example, rising inflation is normally accompanied by rising interest rates; the higher interest rates increase the current and future debt service faced by the government at the same time that they reduce the purchasing power of the outstanding debt. Accordingly, wild inflation is no solution to the deficit problem.

Pass on uneasily to the cyclical deficit, which represents the shortfall of federal revenue as a result of the tax receipts lost when the system and its income flows are operating below a high-employment level. The adjustment has its roots in the high-employment calculations of the early 1960s; it conforms generally to a Keynesian view of the role of "passive," "cyclical" deficits. The result of these calculations thus far, shown on line 9, can be called (also uneasily) the noncyclical or *structural* deficit, representing a mismatch of expenditures and revenues assuming the system is at high employment and already corrected for the elimination of service on the debt accumulated in past deficits.

Finally, and with more practical merit, the deficit may be reduced further by subtracting the measured *investment* outlays of the federal government—an adjustment advanced particularly by those who favor installing a capital account into federal budgeting. This is a reasonable adjustment, and the failure to make it is one of the unhappy distinctions between federal budgeting and business accounting. On the other hand, if we are going to subtract investment outlay from the deficit, should we not add to it some measure of the ongoing depreciation of federally owned physical assets? Bringing this aspect of federal accounting into the logical realm of business accounting would certainly seem to require such an add-back. In any event, simply recording federal outlays of physical facilities has some of its own problems of definition: Should defense facilities (not reflected in table 5–1) be included (they are now running at a rate of about $100 billion)? Should grants-in-aid to state and local governments, largely intended to facilitate physical investment by those governments, be included (they are in the table)? How about "investment" in education and training (about thirty-five billion dollars, not included in the table)?

The deficit thus arrived at on line 11 is by no means necessarily the end of the adjustment process. For example, the expenditures of the Resolution Trust Corporation can be thought of as a loan to that organization to be repaid in the future as the RTC liquidates the assets acquired in refinancing the thrift industry.

It should be obvious that these adjustments (almost all of them invented and used by well-regarded fiscal economists) take the deficit calculation wholly out of the cash-flow concept that appears in line 3, without bringing it toward any other concept recognized in ordinary accounting. Even *naming* the bottom line in table 5–1 calls for an excruciating creative effort.

Let us move on now to the supposed effects of the deficit. In the standard reasoning described above, the financing of a big deficit as appears on line 3 would starve the private system for cash, unless the Federal Reserve were to create the cash to finance it. It would thus seem to pose the threat either of inflation, if the Fed helps a great deal, or recession, if the Federal Reserve withholds its hand and allows the needs of the Treasury to impinge upon a fixed supply of real saving in the capital markets. On the part of those who object to a deficit this size, the point is often made that, while the deficit on line 3 is only 6.8 percent of the GDP, *it is almost half of all of the real saving that goes on in the system.* It is true, of course, that foreigners can export investable funds to the United States, somewhat qualifying the relationship between Federal Reserve behavior and the consequences of the deficit, and this has in fact occurred during most of the years of very large deficits. But that raises numerous other questions, including the question of whether or not such large flows of capital, and the dollar exchange value by which they are mediated, would not themselves add an international debt dimension and might even impair the power of the Federal Reserve to exercise its options on domestic grounds.

This about exhausts the small amount of logic and the large amount of numbers available to examine the issue. Omitted in the discussion are the consequences of changing directions within the spending totals—the immense increase in transfers (mainly "entitlements"), the heavy burden of insurance-type costs now present in the budget, the falling share of real spending, the rising cost of debt service. It is probably true that these alterations in the composition of federal spending have reduced its Keynesian stimulative effect, perhaps very nearly to zero, without benefit of any of the more exotic adjustments described above.

Finally, a quick review of the historical record. Perversely, the size of the cash flow deficit does not seem to be mirrored at all in the consequences. Its financing has not flooded the system with cash; it has occurred in the presence of falling, not rising, inflation and falling, not rising, interest rates.

There is very little evidence that the financing of the deficit has "crowded out" private investment. There is no evidence that the so-called "Ricardian equivalence" theory ("equivalence" because it amounts to saying it makes no difference whether government spending is financed by taxes or by borrowing)—namely, that alert members of the society will recognize budget deficits will require higher taxes of them in the future, and will thus save more in the present (a principle now espoused by modern "rational expectations" theory)—has worked at all. The U.S. personal saving rate has fallen, not risen, in the presence of the deficit. The Keynesians would have expected the deficit to be violently stimulative; no evidence. Supply-siders, who in many respects are responsible for the deficit, given their advocacy of large and continuing tax reductions in the 1980s and even now, are also hard put to find the stimulus they expected. On all of the equivocal aspects of the deficit, the statistical history seems to be strangely silent.

A last observation (to be followed by some conclusions). The term "generational accounting" has been recently introduced as a term to describe longer prospects for the future of the budget burden. The calculations make the point that the federal debt embodied in existing Treasury instruments is only part of the debt that must be financed in the future; the rest of it, more than twice as big as the formally recognized debt, consists of contingent liabilities of the entitlement programs. Inclusion of these liabilities would raise the aggregate obligations of the federal government, to be financed over time, to about eleven trillion dollars. (Most of these incremental liabilities are indexed for inflation, so that not even an "inflation tax" will offset them.) The distribution of these liabilities over time is such as to suggest that the current generation is milking generations of the future, which will confront tax liabilities maybe as much as twenty percent higher, in real terms, than those facing us all today.

Understanding of the budget is thus now hopelessly conflicted; nothing even resembling a consensus is available. It may even be that "generational accounting," which rests in the end on microeconomics rather than Keynesian macroeconomics and pays at least lipservice to Ricardian equivalence, will reshape the whole debate over the next decade. For the present, the following soft conclusions deserve at least qualified acceptance.

In the first place, the cash-flow relationship of the budget to the system, as appears in line 3 of table 5–1, is at least describable as acceptable accounting, although it would be improved by a separation of outlays into consumption and investment, including a depreciation entry. Second, large budget deficits must contain a *tendency* to support or elevate interest rates, particularly long-term rates. Third, while they do conceivably threaten inflation, the risk at present is extremely remote. Fourth, it makes sense to recognize that an underemployed economy costs the federal government in revenues; the passive or cyclical deficit serves a purpose if indeed it were to be stimulative at such times.

Finally, a cash-flow deficit of its present size is, to some unknown degree, an impairment of the system's aggregate saving and thus an impairment of its investment rate. Not much of this can be demonstrated in the realities of the last decade; but it is the fate of economists to have to struggle to deal in isolation with individual theorems whose effects on the real world can be augmented, shrunken, or reversed by large numbers of other very important influences, all at work at the same time. In economics, the *ceteris are never paribus;* the immense statistical effort to hold even a few of them constant rarely yields dependable results. Given the confused state of the statistics, it remains reasonable that a carefully phased reduction of the aggregate deficit would, taken alone, be a favorable influence; and it would act to restore some of the effectiveness of Federal Reserve policies that seek sensitively to achieve a judicious balance between the opposed criteria of growth and inflation.

Monetary Policy

Turn now to the second great arm of national economic policy—the monetary conditions imposed on the system by the Federal Reserve. The Fed, as it is affectionately known to the financial community, is a great and powerful, largely independent (but ultimately a creature of the Congress) system of control over the creation of credit in the system—particularly the commercial banks' power to lend to the private sector and, of course, to government itself.

The creation of credit is a complex and mysterious process, about which not everything is known. This is no place to attempt to describe the process in all its gorgeous obscurity; in any event, only a moderate number of basic propositions are required to explain the figures that the Federal Reserve and the markets issue regularly as a guide to general credit conditions.

Start with the proposition that an enormous flow of funds throughout the system lies beyond the *direct control* of the Federal Reserve. This flow is the so-called real saving generated in the course of economic activity and measured in the national accounts, the saving from which the federal deficit would, in the first instance, be financed. No activity on the part of the Federal Reserve can alter the fact that individuals save, currently at the rate of about $200 billion a year, or that corporations, in an ordinary recent year, experience a gross saving flow of retained earnings and depreciation amounting to about $300 billion a year. These flows would persist and, in ordinary times, would find appropriate investment outlets, altogether apart from the activities of the Federal Reserve System. They are real saving at the absolute disposal of the savers.

The Federal Reserve is concerned with the institutional structure of a financial system capable of engaging in the *creation* of credit. This structure comprises the so-called financial intermediaries, of which the typical and, far and away, the most important is our good friend, the commercial bank. It is the great virtue (and, at times, the great danger) of the commercial banking system that it ordinarily extends an aggregate amount of credit approximately equal to twenty times its own capital. (Some bankers would argue, not without merit, that a well-run bank really requires no capital at all.) The principal function of the Federal Reserve is to regulate the rate of credit creation in the banking system, which can be thought of as the womb of the money supply. No other arm of government can truly create credit; no budget deficits, no lending programs, do anything more than create and augment the demand for credit and alter the direction of credit flows; they do not add to the supply of credit. The Fed reigns over credit availability and hence has much to say about the cost of credit—that is, interest rates.

Credit creation occurs at the imposing desk of a steely eyed banker when he reluctantly accepts the loan instrument of a borrower and creates a bank deposit (a liability of the bank) in return for the debt instrument. The deposit liabilities of the commercial banking system are thus the basic reservoir of money and the place where it is created. The control of this process amounts to a control exercised by the Federal Reserve over the banks' ability to *lend* (the term used in connection with business and consumer loans) and *invest* (the term used in connection with acquisitions of federal, state, and local securities). The control is exercised through the Federal Reserve's application of a *reserve requirement,* by which banks are required to keep at the Federal Reserve a deposit equal to a certain percentage of their deposit liabilities—originally amounting to roughly one-sixth, but recently altered to one-tenth of the demand-type liabilities, and zero percent for most time-deposit-type liabilities.

In the old days, the distinction between demand deposits and time deposits was precise and simple. Commercial banks were essentially depository institutions, accepting demand deposits on a noninterest-bearing basis and time deposits at an interest rate fixed by the Federal Reserve. Massive and rapid deregulation of financial markets generally has produced a proliferation of forms of bank liabilities lying somewhere between demand deposits and time deposits, and banks compete vigorously for varieties of interest-bearing deposits.

Now for a monstrously oversimplified description of the machinery of Federal Reserve control. The Federal Reserve controls the reserves on deposit from commercial banks by *open-market activity*. If it wishes to *expand* the reserves of the banking system, it buys government securities in the open market, ultimately paying for them by *crediting* the reserve position of a commercial bank. The consequence is to put the commercial banks further into an open-to-lend reserve position. If it wishes to *shrink* reserves, it sells government securities on the open market and accepts payment in the form of a debit to the reserve position of a commercial bank. This is an ongoing, continuing process; the Federal Reserve is in the market every day. Its visible behavior in the market is taken as near-conclusive evidence of its attitude toward prevailing interest rates, and, of course, the Fed's *attitude,* even in the absence of action, is itself a significant fact.

The Fed can also achieve the same effects of expansion or constraint on bank reserves (and hence on their ability to lend) by altering the percentage reserve requirements against deposits; it has the power to alter these requirements, as it did in 1992, within ranges set by legislation. A reduction of reserve requirements will free banks to lend more; a rise in reserve requirements will eventually necessitate a contraction of lending.

Finally, the Federal Reserve can make the available credit somewhat more expensive or somewhat cheaper through another device that tends to affect the price of credit. The lending activity of individual banks is a function of their deposits at the Federal Reserve, and the Federal Reserve stands ready to lend reserves to commercial banks seeking to expand their lending beyond the limit of their own reserve position. Reserves so acquired by a commercial bank are called **borrowed reserves** (as distinguished from owned or nonborrowed reserves); the borrowing is from the Federal Reserve, at an interest rate called the **discount rate.** When the Fed lowers the discount rate, it is reducing the banks' cost of borrowed reserves. Since banks customarily borrow little from the Fed, a reduction in the discount rate is, again, more significant as evidence of its attitude than of a real change in the banks' actual cost of funds.

Alternatively, banks in search of a higher reserve position can borrow reserves from other banks blessed with an excess reserve position. There is thus a kind of market in reserves—a *federal funds* market; the interest rate charged by one bank to lend reserves to another bank is known as the **federal funds rate** or, more familiarly, the Fed funds rate. Since borrowing reserves from the Fed and borrowing reserves from other banks are alternatives, the discount rate and the Fed funds rate are competitively related. Normally, the discount rate is modestly lower than the Fed funds rate. The discount rate is an administered rate, a step-function that changes only infrequently by Fed fiat. The federal funds rate is a market rate that changes all the time, as the Fed injects or withdraws reserves through open-market activity. It is generally considered to be the most significant of all short-term rates and the most important economic lever in the hands of the Fed.

Simply for the record, there is one other monetary aggregate that receives close attention, particularly by monetary theorists. This is the **monetary base,** which is the sum of currency in circulation (now about $325 billion) and total reserves of the banking system (now about sixty billion dollars), which would seem to reflect the total potential demand on the economy. But the monetary base is so heavily weighted by its currency component that it tends to be insensitive to dynamic change and has very little real application.

The Condition of Financial Markets

Bearing in mind this simple little edifice of law and custom, it is now possible to take a hard look at the statistics by which all this frantic financial activity can be observed. The deposit liabilities of the banking system; the reserve requirement against those liabilities; the surplus or deficit of the commercial banks' actual reserve, relative to the reserve requirement; the borrowings of commercial banks from the Federal Reserve to meet the reserve requirement; and the outstanding loans and investments of the commercial banking system are all published monthly by the Federal Reserve, and even weekly for an aggregation of large money-center commercial banks (whose behavior is not generally typical of all commercial banks). Changes in the Federal Reserve's discount rate are announced immediately (being an administered rate, it goes for months and sometimes for years without change). The federal funds rate, which for obvious reasons is taken to be an important indicator of how comfortable the supply of reserves really is, is reported continuously all day, every day. (Figure 5–5 shows its behavior in recent years, along with that of the discount rate.) A rise in the federal funds rate is generally taken to mean that bank reserve positions have grown more constrictive, the supply of Fed funds has grown scarcer, and the bidding for them by needy borrowers has grown more intense. Since the actual state of reserves

Figure 5–5. The Cost of Borrowed Reserves

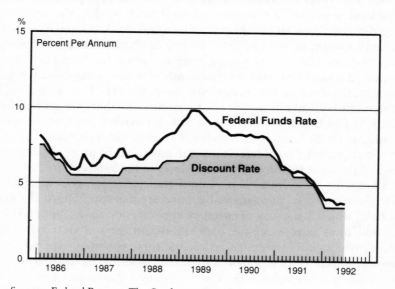

Sources: Federal Reserve; The Conference Board.

is largely controlled by the Fed, movement in the Fed funds rate is an indicator of the mood and intentions of that very important and somewhat secretive institution.

Out of these direct raw materials produced by the ongoing operations of the credit markets, the Federal Reserve derives some fascinating related numbers that are the endless preoccupation of Fed watchers, and of economists in general. Probably the most watched financial statistic is a mysterious number called the **money supply**, which is very sloppily divided into an M_1 money supply and an M_2 money supply (and then an M_3 money supply, and on and on beyond that, even unto L, for all liquid assets). This classification is a series of nesting boxes: M_1, inside M_2, M_2 inside M_3, and so on. The object of this elaborate classification system is to establish definitions of, and then to measure continuously, the supply of money in the system.

There is no easy or handy single definition of *money;* the definitional puzzle has resounded through professional economics ever since it began. Common sense says that *money* is totally liquid, totally negotiable, universally acceptable at face value (although inflation might reduce its real value). The more closely an instrument approximates all these criteria, the more nearly it is money. A ten-dollar bill fits all the requirements, as does a demand deposit—almost. Travelers' checks meet *almost* all the requirements very well, but their negotiability rests on the reputation of the issuer. Checkable deposits that earn interest, as in the case of bank NOW accounts, fit the definition with only a minor delinquency. Such liquid assets are so nearly money as to constitute funds immediately available for spending. In the language of monetary economists, they are *transactions balances,* and their supply is considered to have an immediate relevance for present and prospective spending in the economic system. These components, taken together, constitute M_1, the category that fits most tightly the term *money.*

The biggest single component of M_1 used to be the demand deposits of banks; but currency outstanding is about three-fifths as big as demand deposits, and the so-called other checkable deposits are now bigger than the demand deposits. Taken together, M_1, at this writing, is about $925 billion. Figure 5–6 shows the composition of M_1 in late 1991. The Federal Reserve seeks to control this aggregate and set targets for its proposed growth because very rapid growth would seem to suggest a powerful impending surge in demand and hence an inflationary consequence for the economy as a whole. The Fed's equipment—particularly the open-market activity that controls bank lending and hence the open-to-lend position of the banks reflected in demand deposits—has been directed toward this principal objective. But it takes a borrower, generally, to make M_1, so the Fed's control is really loose and spasmodic rather than continuous.

A second class of money, described in a wild burst of taxonomic creativity as M_2, includes all of M_1, but also what might be called some secondary reserves of money, in the form of smaller time deposits (under $100,000) at

Figure 5–6. The Composition of M₁ Money Stock

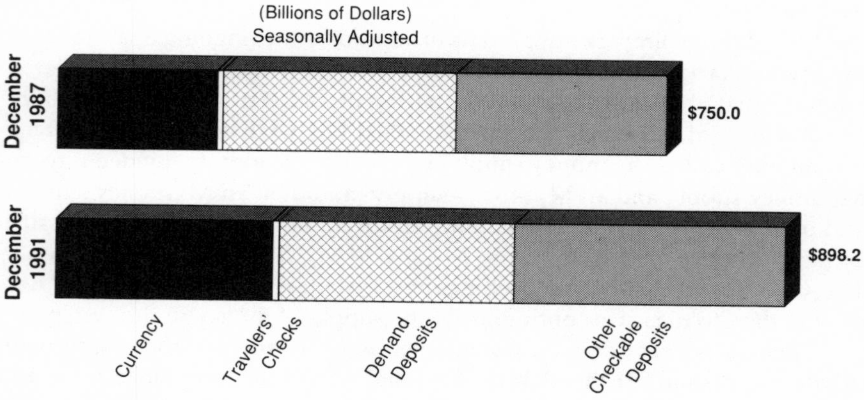

(Billions of Dollars)
Seasonally Adjusted

December 1987 — $750.0

December 1991 — $898.2

Currency   Travelers' Checks   Demand Deposits   Other Checkable Deposits

Sources: Federal Reserve; The Conference Board.

commercial banks and at thrift institutions, and funds in the hands of money-market mutual funds. This somewhat broader measure loses the immediacy of its contact with the economic system because the additional components are thought to have, in some degree, the character of *saving*, rather than a supply of funds intended for prompt spending.

Finally, to M_2 are added large time deposits (over $100,000) and the money market deposits of institutions (also generally large amounts), which are considered to have primarily interest-rate and yield objectives, thus departing still further from a transactions balance. The astute reader will have guessed that this classification is called M_3. Finally, there are a host of other financial instruments—including, among others, savings bonds, short-term Treasury securities, bankers acceptances, and commercial paper—that are near money in many respects but more distant in others. Nevertheless, they are taken to represent forms of liquidity and are, therefore, added to M_3 to produce the ultimate measure of liquid financial assets in the system, known as *L*. Figure 5–7 shows the relative sizes of these various money measures.

More recently, the behavior of M_1 has seemed to suggest that it has become far less relevant, both to the growth of demand in the economic system as a whole, and to the outlook for inflation. Some of the components of M_1 grew at a spectacular rate in 1986 and in late 1991, with little visible consequences for the system. It is widely (and very credibly) argued that the growth of M_1 was a reflection of a general decline in all interest rates and that, as the rates declined, the incentive to move funds out of M_1 into other financial assets was reduced. In other words, the character of M_1 as purely necessary transaction balances was compromised by the deregulation that permitted much of M_1 to earn interest, and then by the reduction of the

Figure 5–7. Definition of Money Stock

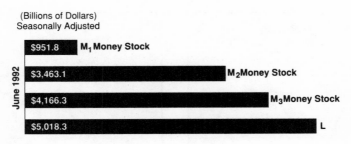

(Billions of Dollars)
Seasonally Adjusted

June 1992

$951.8 — M₁ Money Stock
$3,463.1 — M₂ Money Stock
$4,166.3 — M₃ Money Stock
$5,018.3 — L

Sources: Federal Reserve; The Conference Board.

spread in yields between what could be earned in M_1 forms and what was available outside M_1. In more recent years, the measure has slowed, accelerated, and slowed again, all with no clear reflection in economic activity or inflation.

As a result of these conditions, at least in part, the money statistics began to develop another gross peculiarity. If the money stock is thought of as the supply of funds entering into the transactions included in GDP, then the ratio of the GDP to the money stock becomes a kind of "turnover" rate for the money stock, or (in the turnover term typically used in this connection) a measure of the **velocity** of money. Almost throughout the postwar years, M_1 experienced a gradual increase in velocity of perhaps 2.5 percent per year, reflecting generally rising interest rates and hence more efficient use of the money (faster collections through computerization). The uptrend of velocity was taken to be a basic and dependable component of the money function—until 1982, when the velocity trend was suddenly broken (see figure 5–8). The velocity rose again briefly and then entered on a renewed decline in 1986. It has apparently risen and fallen again since and is still substantially lower than it was six years ago. The now several interruptions of the uptrend in M_1 velocity doubtless reflect the change in the definition of M_1, again because it incorporates interest-bearing accounts in the total. But the velocities of M_2 and even M_3, which have not been importantly altered definitionally, appear to have behaved erratically and undependably over the past several years.

In most of the 1980s, money accordingly seems to have been abundantly available, perhaps even excessively available, given the needs of the slowly growing real economy of the past several years. But the abundance of liquidity, over and above the apparent needs of the real world, seems to have conduced to a fantastic explosion of activity in the financial world (financial transactions in existing assets are not, of course, real output and are, therefore, not included in the GDP). In any event, the enormous multiplications

Figure 5–8. The Erratic Course of Money Velocity

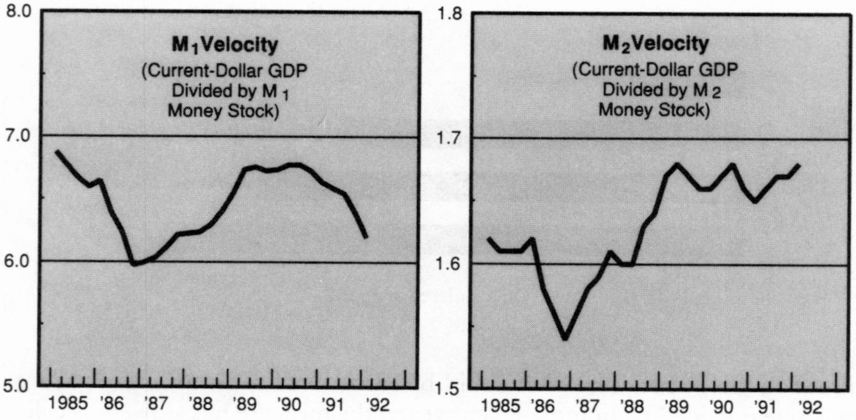

Sources: Federal Reserve; The Conference Board.

of transaction values in financial markets over the past several years (with a huge interruption in 1987) likewise suggest that there is abundant credit available for the real world, when it should call for it; and, in turn, this suggests that the existing stock of money is not now a hindrance to fast growth in the system, and that it might even be adequate to support a rising rate of inflation. For these reasons, the chairman of the Federal Reserve, Alan Greenspan, appears to subscribe very fully to the views of his distinguished predecessor, Paul Volcker, in considering inflation still to be an important, although at mid-1992 certainly not immediate, threat to U.S. economic stability. If it can be said that there was a "money crunch" affecting the economy in recent years, it has resulted not from an inadequacy of bank reserves, but extreme caution on the part of the banks in lending to the private sector, reflecting their immense losses on real estate loans, and equal caution on the part of overextended borrowers.

The behavior of M_1 and M_2 can also be studied in relationship to the real output of the system and the inflation rate of the system. In the first instance, the money stock, divided by a measure of output, yields a figure that reflects, speaking broadly, the number of dollars in the system chasing each unit of goods and, hence, some indication of the inflation pressure in the system. A second measure, achieved by dividing the money stock figures by a measure of inflation, produces numbers that might be called the *real* purchasing power of the money stock and, hence, some guide to the prospective real growth rate of the system. These rather useful statistics, which appear in figure 5–9, on the whole display the same problems visible in the untreated money stock figures; that is, their logical relevance to the issues of inflation and growth are not very clearly revealed in the actual history.

Figure 5–9. The Adjusted Behavior of the Money Stock

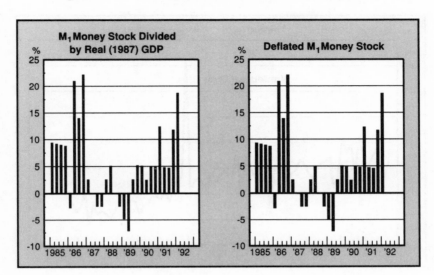

Sources: Federal Reserve; The Conference Board.

The classification of M_1, running to L, is built on the measurement of financial assets. For every financial asset (except equities) there is, of course, a financial debt. (For some debts—long-term debts of governments, corporate bond indebtedness, indebtedness on mortgages—the financial instrument that constitutes the asset is so long-term and so open to fluctuation in the course of its existence that it is quite properly not considered to be *money* at all.) In recent years, the Federal Reserve has accordingly constructed a debt aggregate that covers the obligations (as distinguished from the assets) of all domestic nonfinancial sectors, including all obligations of government. The rate of growth of this aggregate debt figure is of intense interest itself; its components are reported in considerable detail in the quarterly Federal Reserve publication called "Flow of Funds," but monthly estimates are also published by the Federal Reserve. Figure 5–10 shows the growth rate of this debt aggregate in recent years.

All these measures of money constitute a definition of *money* from its narrowest to its broadest conception All the definitions are of significance to the Federal Reserve and to the financial markets and therefore, to businesspersons and investors. Although the Federal Reserve's control over this structure is heavily concentrated in the components that directly involve the extension of bank credit, its influence radiates across all the other categories, for a powerful and important reason. As indicated earlier, the interest rates available throughout the entire range of securities are tied together by the inevitable arbitrage among them. If the Federal Reserve uses its power to

Figure 5–10. The Rise and Fall of Debt Growth

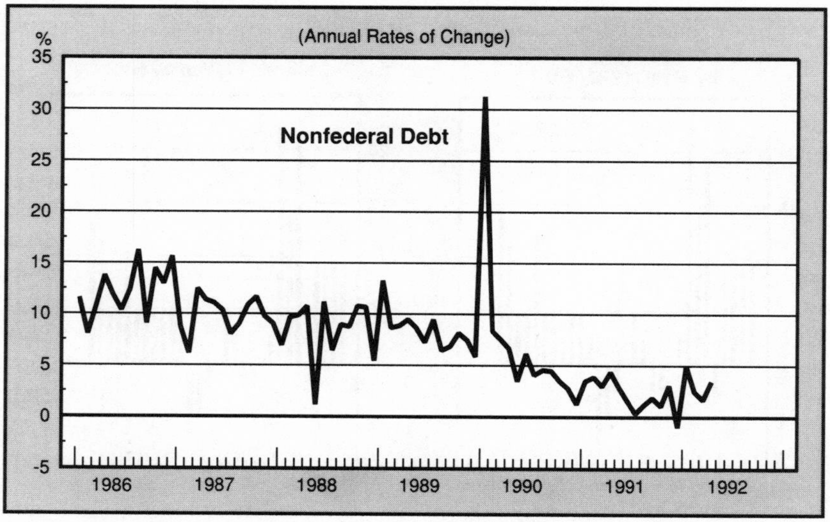

Sources: Federal Reserve; The Conference Board.

make bank reserves less available, the inevitable consequence is higher interest rates in short-term securities markets. Such higher short-term rates compete with all other forms in which liquidity can be carried; hence, they drive up yields in parts of the structure not directly controlled by the Federal Reserve, as the whole structure seeks a competitive equilibrium. In general, the interest rates throughout this structure tend to move together, although short-term rates normally move faster and farther than do long-term rates, in which other influences, principally attitudes toward prospective inflation playing exclusively on segments of the whole structure, can produce a pattern of cross-trends. In the first half of 1992, short-term rates fell because business was weak, demand for credit was weak, and the Federal Reserve was relatively accommodative; at the same time, continuing fears of inflation—the *bete noir* of long-term investors—offset the decline in short rates and yields remained very high. The interest rates that have prevailed among various parts of the money spectrum are seen in figure 4–12, which shows the *yield curve* of Treasury securities at several points in time.

Now, some final words on the integration of these two immensely powerful economic instruments in the hands of the federal government. An earlier section treated a large federal budget deficit, accounted for as a cash flow, as stimulative in a first-round analysis. It is stimulative because the federal government issues risk-free securities to obtain its necessary increment of cash and then spends the cash, leaving the rest of the system with all the cash it had in the first place, plus an increment of risk-free securities that are very nearly cash in the eyes of the holder. At the moment that the government seeks its cash, however, it is competing for the attention of investors, to capture part of the real saving that is going on in the system all the time; if it wins in the competition, it is depriving the private sector of access to that portion of the ongoing saving. And it always does win, for the simple reason that it *must* borrow and, therefore, pays whatever the going interest rate may be. Unlike the private sector, government borrowing is "rate-insensitive." It is thus tapping the *real* saving of the system, reducing the availabilities to other borrowers, and presumably driving up the interest rates that other borrowers will have to pay. The consequence does not increase the money supply and poses no threat of inflation as long as the government's needs are met out of the real saving, as it is, for example, in such high-saving economies as Japan and Germany; that would simply mean that the government would grow, while the growth of the private sector would be inhibited by lesser credit at higher rates—that is, the private sector would be "crowded out" of the credit markets. If business were in recession at the time, its need for credit might be very low, and the financing of the federal deficit would have no consequences not already imposed by recession itself.

However—a big however—in an effort to accommodate the demands of the Treasury, there are many things the Federal Reserve can do. It can make banks very open to lending by elevating their reserves, in which case the banks themselves could buy a lot of the new Treasury securities, relieving the private nonfinancial sector of a need to do so and forestalling any rise in interest rates. (That is about what has happened in 1991 and 1992.) The Fed would do this by direct open-market activity, buying some of the Treasury securities itself. A large part—perhaps even all—of the issues of Treasury securities to cover the debt could thus be placed with the Federal Reserve and the commercial banks. When the commercial banks buy the securities, they pay for them by crediting the Treasury's accounts; in this sense, they are creating money in the same way they do when they accept a private borrower's loan instrument and credit his account with a deposit liability. The result, of course, is to expand the *M* measures of money through creation of credit.

This process—often called *monetization of debt*—is generally considered temporarily desirable (certainly at least excusable) in the course of a recession, when the whole system is underemployed and increases in credit for both government and the private sector appear to be desirable stimuli. But when the private sector is doing very well, thank you, and is urgently seeking credit for its own expansive views of its future, the Federal Reserve is naturally less inclined to add fuel to what may in the end be an inflationary fire. If it does not accommodate the borrowing requirements of the Treasury to finance the deficit, it will force the financing onto the private sector at a time when the private sector has a lot of its own financing to do. The aggregate **demand for credit**—the debt variable that the Federal Reserve watches—would grow rapidly if the Federal Reserve were to be accommodative under such circumstances; if it is not accommodative, the federal borrowing needs will compete (occasionally violently, as in 1981 and 1982) with the borrowing needs of the private sector, and the whole structure of interest rates will rise. Since the federal government borrows when it needs to, regardless of interest rates, in the end, it will be the private sector that will be priced out. Those demands in the private sector that are heavily dependent on credit—purchases of major consumer durables, purchases of plant and equipment, and housing construction in particular—will suffer. The inventory policies of business will grow more conservative on account of the high interest cost of carrying the inventory.

In conventional reasoning, a big budget deficit is thus stimulative to the economy *only* if it is accommodated by monetary policy—that is, *only* if the Federal Reserve will meet the demand of the deficit as well as the aggregate private demand. It is *not* stimulative if the Federal Reserve refuses to accommodate the demand. A big deficit and a restrictive, nonaccommodative monetary policy are thus operating in conflict; indeed, they operated in just such conflict throughout the early 1980s, when outcomes for interest rates and for economic activity were extremely cyclical and destabilizing. While recessions always have multiple causes, the enormous interest rates of 1981 were the preponderant reason for the major recession of 1981–1982.

Such dramatic conflicts in the applications of economic policy often have substantial side-effect consequences, and the consequences are often difficult to foresee. In the early 1980s, the enormous appetite of the federal government for credit was an invitation to capital all over the world. The road to investment in the United States inevitably ran headlong through the market for the dollar, raising it far above its value as measured in conventional purchasing-power terms and impairing the merchandise trade position of the United States, where it precipitated a flood of imports. Further description of this machinery is reserved for chapter 6, but here it might be noted that the huge surge of imported goods into the United States that reflected the high dollar also suppressed American inflation, with the peculiar and unpredictable result that a huge deficit in the federal budget occurred in the presence of a major decline in the inflation rate—a neat, and for once explicable, economic paradox.

The conflicted, irresolute, theoretically impracticable condition that beset the economic policy in the 1980s is thus not an accident, and it does not simply reflect bureaucratic stupidity; it cannot even be blamed on the huge uncertainties affecting fiscal outcomes and their consequences, as described above. The budget deficit that exists today, and seems to impend for the next several years, in part reflects decisions of government to enhance U.S. incentives to work and invest through reduction of tax rates. The Federal Reserve, on the other hand, accepts its commitment to provide credit for growth of the economy; but it is acutely aware of the proposition, accepted by almost all economists, that very rapid growth of money—faster than the probable growth rate of real activity in the economy—threatens to bid up prices and turn the system toward a high and destructive general inflation. The joint target of the two arms of policy can be said to be a vigorously growing economy with considerable new investment for efficiency and growth in the future, a relatively low level of unemployment, and relatively stable prices. Economic outcomes are very hard to predict, however, and events not controlled by either of the two arms of policy often intervene to upset even the most careful calculations and to drive the system away from one or several of the agreed target conditions. Doubtless the federal government—the administration and the Congress as well—would be eager to seek a lower cash-flow deficit, requiring less financing; the Federal Reserve would doubtless prefer to see lower interest rates—particularly the long-term rates that influence housing and capital spending—and slower growth in public debt. The figures charted in this chapter, on the condition of the federal budget and federal debt, and on the money stock and the rate of growth of debt, frame an unresolved issue for the rest of the decade.

6

The United States in the World

T he United States is far and away the world's largest national economy. Its geographical size, and its wide range of climate and of soils,
together with its isolation from the rest of the developed world,
have made it, throughout its history, a uniquely independent nation, requiring little from others. The huge size and rapid growth of its domestic market
have provided ample opportunity to its native industries. Its open border
with Canada and its partly common heritage have produced, for a century,
substantial volumes of trade with its northern neighbor; as for the rest, the
United States historically had almost the smallest international sector of any
of the developed economies.

This high degree of independence, bordering on economic isolation, has
been fundamentally altered in the postwar years, to the point where it is no
longer really possible to understand U.S. economic experience without reference to its large and growing—and troubled—linkages with the rest of the
world. Chapter 1 reviewed the progressive involution of the U.S. international position as an element in the long history of its postwar wave of
growth and subsidence. In any event, the trade flows, the investment flows,
and the financial and currency flows that tie the United States to its trading
partners are now of such dramatic importance that they exert large influences on even the most determinedly domestic business operations in the
United States.

International economics, a highly developed specialty within the general
field, has many complicated things to say about the nature of international
markets and the international consequences of domestic economic policies.
In this area, the disputes among the specialists are particularly intense, running even to the very nature of international economic adjustment.

In general, theory views the international market as a great opportunity
for improvement in world output and living standards. As long as the system
refrains from barriers to trade, "comparative advantage," expressed under
conditions of "free trade," is good for all. It also views the world market as
a discipline on the performance of individual economies; to put it as simply

138

as possible, highly stimulative misbehavior at home, in the unwise pursuit of domestic happiness, will be judged and punished in the world market. The eating of domestic substance shrinks exports, draws in imports, and reduces the value of the currency relative to other currencies because it grows so abundant abroad in payment for the excesses of imports. The decline of the currency elevates the cost of imports and contributes an international component to the inflation that domestic misbehavior would cause in any event. In the hoary days of the gold standard, substantial international deficits drew down a nation's gold supply, shrinking the base of its currency, threatening credit stringency and serious recession. In free-market international theory, crime (improvident behavior at home) still begets punishment—inflation if the currency weakens, recession if imported goods flood the domestic market.

Simply put, this is the great retributive mechanism of international economics. The United States has been a dominant and powerful economy in the world for a long time; and the respect accorded to it (and to its currency), as well as its near self-sufficiency in almost everything, and its technological lead for much of its history, freed it from the iron laws of international economics. But as chapter 1 pointed out at length, the circumstances on which this proud isolation was based have now very largely disappeared. Advanced technology has been spread all around the world (in part, by the foreign investment of U.S. companies), where it is often combined with labor costs far lower than our own. The U.S. dollar, formerly held in enormously high regard, is, nevertheless, no longer convertible into gold as it was during the twenty-five years of the gold-exchange standard developed at Bretton Woods; and its value relative to other currencies now fluctuates in a floating-rate regime. In the 1980s, in particular, the dollar soared early in the decade in response to towering interest rates in the United States; since about the middle of the decade, it has fallen all the way back to about its value as the decade began. Accompanying this immense wave in the dollar's value has been a comparable wave in the U.S. trade position—deteriorating dramatically in the early years of the decade as the high value of the currency elevated the cost of U.S. exports to our trading partners and greatly reduced the costs of imports in the United States and recovering almost as rapidly as the dollar fell back to its pre-1980's level. The United States is now a substantial exporter of both agricultural goods and manufacturing goods; it is also the world's biggest importer.

As a consequence of the huge volume of trade deficits in the 1980s, a staggering amount of dollar assets exist in the world markets—a reflection of the outflow of dollars in payment for the excess of U.S. imports over its exports. By 1987, the United States had become the biggest net debtor in the world as it settled its bumper-sized trade deficits in dollars that represent claims on U.S. output. For the United States, this is a new, tough ball game, its risks compounded by the virtually total internationalization of financial markets (with their capacity for gigantic volumes of financial transfers at electronic speed) and further compounded by the enormous potential inflows and outflows of dollars held by foreign nationals. The risks in our international accounts are now too big to be ignored by any U.S. industry, however isolated it may be from direct international competition.

The basic concept in the measurement of international economic relations, similar in some ways to the national accounts for domestic economics, for decades, was called the **balance of payments**—an aggregate measure of the flows of goods and services between the United States and its multiple trading partners. The form of this accounting system has changed over the years, as the international currency arrangements have changed. In today's world of floating currencies detached from gold, attention focuses most particularly on what is called the **current account**, whose surplus or deficit is inevitably settled in dollars.

The current account records all international sales—of services as well as goods—between the United States and its trading partners. Its principal components are merchandise exports and imports (the difference is called the *trade balance*); tourism outlays of U.S. travelers abroad, less the outlays of foreign travelers in the United States; the investment income earned by U.S. investment abroad, less the investment earnings of others on their investment in the United States; and travel, passenger fares, and other transportation receipts, less expenditures on such services provided by foreigners. Only the merchandise trade portion of the account is available monthly; the whole account is prepared quarterly by the U.S. Department of Commerce.

The net exports line in the gross domestic product, which is the national-accounts reflection of much of this activity, is approximately the equivalent of the current account. (Both series can bounce around dramatically in response to unusual flows; for example, the immense inflows as foreign nations paid their obligations to help finance the Gulf War in early 1991.) The major components of the current account are shown in figure 6–1, which reveals the deficit on the part of the U.S. **merchandise balance** and a partially offsetting surplus on the so-called *invisibles*—the nontrade tourism and investment flows. The exports and imports entering into the current account are available monthly in total and in very fine detail by commodity and by trading partner. The aggregate U.S. trade position and the position relative to four major trading partners are shown in figure 6–2. Figure 6–3 shows exports and imports in three major commodity groups: capital goods, in which the U.S. runs a surplus, and autos and other consumer goods, in which the U.S. runs deficits. A third large deficit, not shown separately, relates to our massive petroleum importation. In virtually all other major commodity categories, U.S. trade is now in balance or in surplus.

The merchandise trade pattern shown in figure 6–2 is the ultimate reflection of several conditions; the present deficit illustrates all of them. In the

Figure 6–1. The U.S. International Accounts

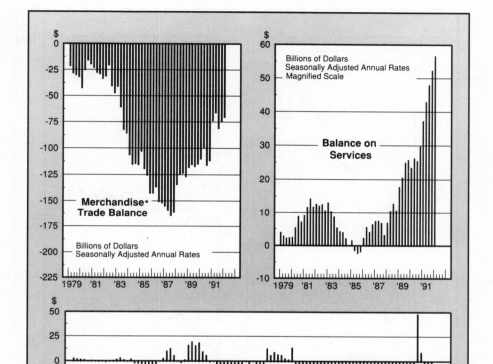

*Excluding transfers under military grants.

▲Including net unilateral transfers not shown separately.

Sources: U.S. Department of Commerce; The Conference Board.

Figure 6–2. The U.S. Trade Position

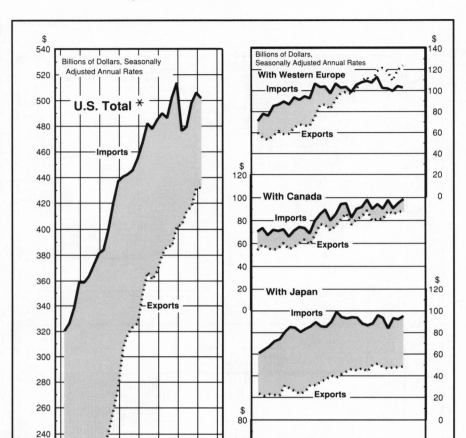

*Includes countries, or areas, not shown separately.
Sources: U.S. Department of Commerce; The Conference Board.

Figure 6–3. Merchandise Exports and Imports, by Type of Product

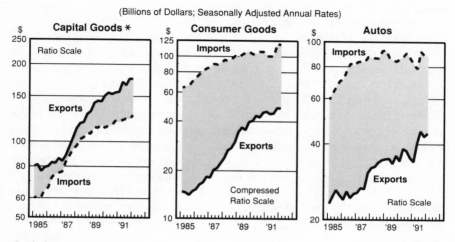

(Billions of Dollars; Seasonally Adjusted Annual Rates)

*Excluding autos.

Sources: U.S. Department of Commerce; The Conference Board.

first place, from 1983 to 1989, the United States experienced a faster expansion in aggregate domestic demand than appeared among many of its trading partners; our market for the exports of others grew much faster than their markets for our exports. Second, the immense advance in the exchange value of the dollar from 1980 to early 1985 meant that foreign products appeared to be relatively cheap (even though their prices were rising in terms of their own domestic currencies, the dollar commanded much more of their currencies). Conversely, the high dollar meant that it took much more foreign currency to buy U.S. products. Our exports were thus shrunken by their higher costs, while imports were stimulated by their lower costs. The intersection, in the middle 1980s, of a very high dollar and relatively fast growth in domestic demand, produced mammoth growth in imports, a world-record trade deficit, and a violent outflow of dollars to settle the imbalance. In recent years, of course, the currency effect has reversed with a vengeance, and exports have grown far faster than imports, substantially reducing the trade gap. Nonetheless, exporters to the United States have clung very competitively to the market positions developed during the years of the high dollar.

The spread of advanced technology, even into developing countries where labor costs are dramatically lower than in the United States (and where the domestic propensity to consume is very low), has also created a whole new range of low-cost competitors. Finally—and, as history may write, perhaps more importantly—the Pacific Basin (Japan, South Korea,

Taiwan, Hong Kong, Singapore) has witnessed an explosion of output among countries with spectacularly low propensities for domestic consumption. This powerful independent reason for the U.S. trade dilemma, of course, augments all the other reasons.

Given the enormous supply of dollars already existing around the world, and the increment to the supply that has resulted from settlement of our current-account deficit, one would expect (that is, international economic theory would argue) that the U.S. dollar should have been weak, not strong, even into 1985. Figure 6–4 reveals how phenomenally strong it was. Not everything is known about why it was so strong, but at least some of the reasons are clear. With a burgeoning recovery that required a lot of credit to sustain it, with a very large budget deficit requiring financing, and with a Federal Reserve that remained studiously alert to any excesses in the provision of created credit, U.S. interest rates were strikingly high in the first half of the 1980s. The high interest rates available in the United States made dollar investments here particularly attractive, and the demand for dollars for this purpose was enormous. The outflow of dollars resulting from the need to settle our international deficits seemed to make a quick U-turn, returning to our own shores for investment at interest rates that exceeded those available in most of the rest of the world. This investment opportunity was reinforced by the prevailing view that the dollar is a safe currency—a haven against the political and economic vicissitudes that may well beset less

Figure 6–4. The Course of the Dollar

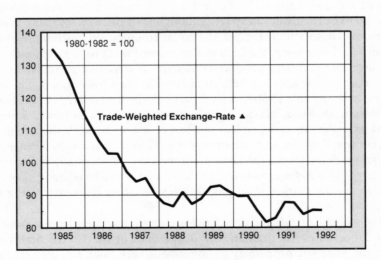

▲Based on pre-June 1970 parities.
Sources: Morgan Guaranty Trust Company; The Conference Board.

vigorous or less stable economies and their currencies. The huge dollar-exchange market—doubtless by a vast multiple the biggest market in the world, and almost totally unsupervised—thus had a wonderful product; among the safest currencies anywhere and among the highest-yielding investments. Thus the outflow of dollars returned as an inflow—now, of course, owned by nationals of other countries. This is the common form of the statement. The impression it conveys is not wrong; but in actuality, the dollars involved never leave the United States. Instead, the ownership of the dollars changes hands from a U.S. national to a foreign holder as the imports are paid for by a check on a U.S. bank. Such dollars, called balance-of-payments dollars, are also inextinguishable; they can be reduced only by a surplus in the U.S. current account. There are, of course, other dollars that can be brought to bear on the U.S. by foreigners borrowing Eurodollars abroad. These dollars carry a liability side; they can grow and subside as they are created and extinguished.

The accumulating reinvestment of foreign-owned dollars in the United States in most of the 1980s was so massive that it eroded the U.S. net investment position throughout the world and converted the U.S. international asset position from a net creditor to a formidably large net debtor position (see figure 1–5). Even the surplus that the United States has always earned on its physical investment abroad, which was about thirty billion dollars at the start of the decade, disappeared entirely by 1989. It has since recovered slightly.

The international dilemma of huge dollar holdings abroad is traceable to a set of sequential anomalies in the U.S. economic situation in the years 1981 to 1985; a very high budget deficit conducive to very high interest rates, which in turn is conducive to a substantial trade deficit. The payment remains in the United States, attracted by the high interest rates, and, as a form of saving, helps in some degree to finance the budget deficit that stands at the beginning of this train of consequences. The dollar exchange value in 1984 was, by general agreement, far too high on a purchasing-power basis; the evidence for that conclusion is the trade deficit itself. But the international economic consequences that would normally follow—a flooding of the world with unwanted dollars, hence, a decline in the value of the dollar and a return toward equilibrium in the trade position—were forestalled by the combination of loose fiscal policy (big deficits requiring financing) and firm monetary policy (restricted supply of credit and, hence, high interest rates).

From early 1985 far into 1989, the value of the dollar, relative to the currencies of other major developed economies, fell very sharply indeed. By mid-1987, the currency adjustment had progressed to the point where U.S. production costs were actually lower in many industries than they were in Germany and Japan. Exports had begun to grow again, and the importation rate appeared to have stabilized. But the issue is far from resolved. Some markets for U.S. exports have dwindled, in more than a short-term sense. The OPEC countries can no longer buy U.S. output with the abandon they could afford in the late 1970s. U.S. agriculture is probably the most efficient in the world, but other countries that were major importers of U.S. farm products are approaching self-sufficiency. The newly industrializing countries (South Korea, Taiwan, Hong Kong, Singapore, and now spectacularly, mainland China) address themselves to U.S. markets (the most attractive, of course, in the world) equipped with state-of-the-art technology and far lower labor costs. Finally, the United States has emerged into a high-consumption, low-saving, high-deficit phase of its history. Perhaps the saddest statistics of the 1980s were the high rate of importation of other countries' savings and the application of these savings to the financing of the federal deficit—in effect, to consumption purposes in the United States. For the U.S. businessperson, whether heavily involved in international trade or not, these considerations pose one of the great issues of the 1990s. They clearly were among the root causes of the collapse of the U.S. equity market in late 1987 and the very hesitant recovery from recession experienced in 1991 and early 1992.

It should be added that in the last few years the nature of this issue has changed importantly and, on the whole, for the better. After its intense suffering during the period of the exalted dollar, manufacturing industry in the United States has made a substantial adjustment to the world market. At the value of the dollar that prevailed in mid-1992, it now competes on at least equal terms with its major industrial competitors, and the subdued price of oil has reduced this major loss category in the trade accounts (despite rising importation measured in barrels). Its services incomes have also continued to grow quite respectably—to about a thirty billion dollar surplus in late 1991. The entire current account is thus vastly improved from the conditions prevailing when the last edition of this book went to press. On the other hand (the reader may have encountered this phrase from economists before), the related inflow of capital from the rest of the world has also subsided; the financing of a budget deficit now even bigger than in 1987 is thus much more dependent on the collection of indigenous capital—that is, the U.S. indigenous saving rate. The shortfall in the availability of foreign capital, in the presence of continued massive federal financing, tends to keep U.S. interest rates higher than they would otherwise be and higher (particularly at the long end of the yield curve) than the Federal Reserve or domestic investors would wish. As the international accounts have improved, the locus of these problems has shifted toward the saving propensities of the U.S. system—an issue taken up in great detail in chapter 8. But for financial markets, the huge foreign holdings of dollars abroad and in the U.S. bear heavily and unpredictably on the capital markets and on U.S. interest rates. Among the crucial aspects of every new major Treasury financing, which now runs to nearly forty billion dollars each quarter, the behavior of Japanese investors ranks as a central concern, in that a reduced purchase by Japan threatens to elevate U.S. rates.

A last issue; in a globalized market for goods and services, the world's major economies can react to substantial changes in the trade performance of the U.S. Others prospered mightily as U.S. imports rose in the late 1980s: As our own adjustment proceeded in the late 1980s and early 1990s, our trading partners' growth performance began to slow. In the usual circularity of economics, the slowing of growth among these economies is now slowing the growth of our own export markets. We are, in truth, now a component of a world market; and in 1992, lacking any nation capable of acting as a locomotive for the whole, the whole world has slowed.

7

Inflation and Economic Policies

A long with unemployment (which, in many respects, is its obverse manifestation), inflation is one of the great enemies of a market economy. Inflation, actual or anticipated, is a mover of business judgment, a powerful influence on consumer attitudes, a displacer of our international position, a major concern of economic policy. An understanding of it is essential to reasoned appraisal of the U.S. outlook. Understanding it isn't easy, however.

As with any other important variable in a complex structure, the rate of inflation is both a consequence of and a causal influence on the behavior of the system as a whole. Changes in the inflation rate, for whatever reason, have significant effects on aggregate economic performance; they also have important distributive effects, altering the fortunes of debtors and creditors and producing differential consequences between importers and exporters, consumption industries and investment industries, and holders of goods and holders of financial instruments.

These differential consequences make inflation a contentious political subject—all the more so since the causes of changes in the inflation rate are themselves a matter of dispute. Embedded as it is in a broad range of intense self-interest issues close to the hearts of various segments of the electorate, inflation in its elevated phases becomes a center of political and even philosophical debate that occasionally approaches religious intensity, clouding its real significance for business. In the early 1970s and again in the late 1970s, inflation control became the overriding criterion of policy, superseding job creation, growth, and cyclical stability, even though its principal cause—the explosion of oil prices attributable to the behavior of OPEC—lay beyond the control of U.S. policy.

By virtue of their supposed consequences for inflation, the two principal instruments of economic policy—the management of money and credit and the management of the federal budget—acquire powerful emotive significance that is played on, often in an alarming way, in the political process. Fiscal policies and monetary policies, however, affect much more than just the inflation rate; they influence employment, economic growth, credit availability to consumers and investors, the services provided by government, and the burden of government costs resting on the private sector. To understand the U.S. price environment and to grasp its future, it seems essential that we seek a practical, nondoctrinal appraisal of the record in the United States, and of the causes that have led to the consequences, if we are to arrive at realistic and sustainable relationships between the inflation rate and the many other criteria by which our economic performance is judged.

We should first recognize that the character of inflation changes as the rate rises. The difference between the inflation rate experienced in the 1970s and the two-percent average rate experienced in the 1950s is not simply a matter of numbers; it is profoundly qualitative. At some point between the two experiences, inflation changes its character so dramatically as to invite an altogether different appraisal—even, one might think, a different name. A high rate of inflation colors the real world with expectational speculative incentives that distort behavior and sap real activity by diverting attention to balance-sheet concerns, investment decisions acquire complex new dimensions, and incentives to save deteriorate unless offset by interest rates so high as to impede real growth and to devalue such balance-sheet assets as housing. The capricious and inequitable distribution of the burden of inflation intensifies the distributive struggle over shares of output, while the search for parochial shelter from inflation often accentuates the general rate. An elevated rate of inflation also tends to generate a stream of policy decisions and institutional adjustments that are not necessarily desirable on other grounds and may, in fact, be self-defeating.

Inflation is not, in itself, subject to ethical characterization; it is not inherently good or bad. The rate is undesirably high when adverse economic consequences can be shown to ensue, or to be probable. An inflation rate *not* accompanied by (or threatening to produce) such consequences may not be theoretically beautiful, but its treatment should be subordinated to the many other criteria by which economic performance should be judged—particularly the criteria of job creation, living standards, and the rate of private investment.

Economic policy can certainly accelerate inflation. One need not subscribe to doctrinal monetarism to agree that there are rates of creation of money and credit so substantially faster than the growth of actual and potential output as to be conducive to a too-high aggregate and general rate of inflation, at least for a time. One need not be religious about the desirability of balancing the federal budget to accept the conclusion that large and prolonged federal deficits (like what we have lived with for a decade) complicate life for a central bank charged with the responsibility for avoiding high inflation; in the end, its alternatives become financing an undesirable rate of inflation or driving interest rates to levels that will depress the private economy as a whole, and its investment function in particular. Ultimately, economic policy is made by our elected representatives—the administration and the Congress. Even a supposedly independent central bank has no real mandate to maintain an anti-inflation posture beyond the point where the interest-rate consequences for economic performance become violently depressive, as measured by unemployment, living standards, and investment rates. Budget deficits are too high, and ultimately inflationary, when they impose these alternatives on the central bank.

Although policy can cause inflation, the historical record of monetary policy and fiscal policy in the United States displays a considerable conservative sensitivity to the threat of inflation. The actual record of the growth of credit in the United States—and, until the 1980s, the actual record of federal deficits—by no means suggests improvident policymaking. Nor does the record of the inflation rate itself in the United States suggest a persistent or systematic loss of control over the U.S. price level. The record in the United States lends little support to the conclusion that we have brought inflation on ourselves by persistent policy mistakes. Indeed, the record of the 1980s, which featured a massive wave of debt formation in both the federal and nonfederal sectors (see figure 7–1), all in the presence of a declining inflation rate, suggests that the U.S. economy is now surprisingly resistant to inflation.

The long history of the money stock in the United States, relative to the aggregate gross domestic product (all expressed in current dollars) hardly suggests a clear causal relationship to inflation. Most measures of money and credit availability appear to have grown modestly over the long term and less rapidly than the GDP itself—a reflection of increasing "efficiency" in the use of money, in turn, attributable in part to revolutionary improvement in data processing and communication. The volume of M_1 is far below the relative levels of ten or fifteen years ago. In fact, if M_1 were to be adjusted by the inflation rate itself, its real volume still appears no higher than fifteen years ago.

It is true that waves in the growth rate of money are correlated with ensuing waves in price statistics—a point on which monetarists rest their statistical case—but the correlation operates only under conditions of abnormal and spectacular departures from trend. In any event, the availability of credit is an influence not just on the price level, but on the volume of real activity as well. Simple correlation of money growth with inflation overflies the normal sequence of causality that any businessperson will recognize— the trail runs from money, to real markets, to strained resources, to prices. The cyclical rise and fall in the strength of markets should certainly be given some weight in explanation of price behavior. In its periodic ventures into relatively rapid money growth (as, for example, in the last half of 1982 and in late 1991), the Federal Reserve has generally reacted to the legitimate and understandable need to improve economic performance as measured by such real criteria as the unemployment rate and the trend of real investment.

Figure 7–1. The Explosion of Debt in the 1980s

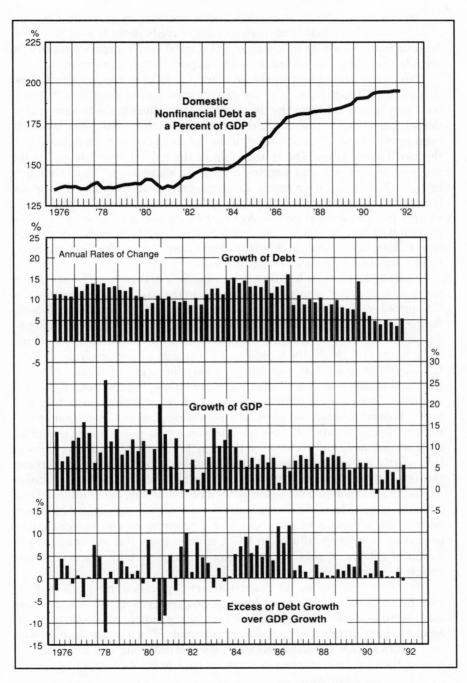

Sources: Federal Reserve; U.S. Department of Commerce; The Conference Board.

In any event, the issue is not whether money can cause inflation (of course it can), but whether the management of credit in the United States has been such as to identify it as a clear, substantial, and independent cause of the inflation itself. The record does not support such an argument.

Much the same point might be made for federal budgets and federal deficits. Until recently, most of the deficits experienced since World War II were very largely explained by the response of revenues to the business cycle; the structural, active, noncyclical component of the deficits has generally been small. The structural portion of the deficit has often been in surplus in the past twenty years. The relationship of the federal debt (viewed as the accumulation of past and ongoing deficits) to aggregate GDP, as shown in figure 5–2, subsided from nearly 1.0 in the early years, to under 0.35 in the late 1970s; it rose dramatically in the 1980s, but inflation nevertheless fell sharply throughout that period. Again, the issue is not whether deficits *can* cause inflation, but whether the *actual* deficits have been such as to constitute a clear, substantial, and independent cause. Again, the long historical record does not support such an argument.

Indeed, the postwar history of inflation itself in the United States carries the same suggestion of moderate behavior. In the past twenty-five years, the U.S. price level has certainly experienced several serious accelerations of inflation, but they appear to have been related more to energy prices than to any permanent bias of policy toward inflation in the United States (see figure 7–2). In the late 1960s, the build-up of a war that so hopelessly divided the U.S. people as to forestall and delay ordinary financing, produced a kind of guns-and-butter crisis with inflationary potentials; but the potentials were contained by two comparatively moderate surges of interest rates tolerated by the Federal Reserve and ultimately by a temporary tax. A second escalation, beginning in late 1972 (as the Nixon incomes-policy effort was gradually abandoned) and continuing through 1973, appears to have been at least partly related to a general coincidence of business-cycle expansions throughout the West, in the presence of a rapidly developing Eurodollar market that contributed the liquidity for a near doubling of the international commodity price level. This experience was immensely aggravated by an unprecedented elevation of oil prices and a pronounced rise in agricultural prices caused by crop failures. In 1979, another lesser but still dramatic elevation of oil prices, together with another surge in farm prices, restored double-digit inflation.

In all these instances, the Federal Reserve appears to have behaved circumspectly in the exercise of its domestic powers, even though it necessarily confronted *international* inflation by curbing the supply of *domestic* credit, elevating interest rates, and producing recession. When international recession followed U.S. domestic recession, the inflation rate was reduced, and the Fed then inevitably turned its attention back to the stimulation of domestic recovery and growth.

Figure 7–2. Consumer Prices and The Explosion in Energy Prices

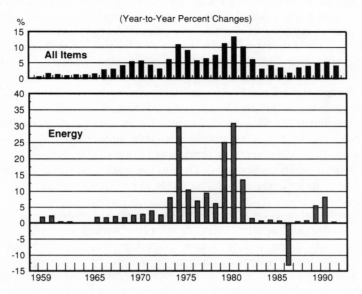

Sources: U.S. Department of Labor; The Conference Board.

Monetarism may argue that if monetary policy were not to have accommodated such surges in the price level in their early stages, they could not have occurred; that is, under a strict monetary regime, the rise in the prices of the directly affected commodities (petroleum products, food) would have been offset by falling prices for other commodities, producing *relative* price change but not *aggregate* inflation. This argument assumes a perfectly fluid equilibrium market system, perfectly mobile resources, and perfectly flexible prices in predominantly auction markets; the assumptions are fatally unrealistic. Much of the extraordinary inflation experience of the 1970s, and much of the instability of interest rates in that decade, is owing not to misbehavior of economic policymakers, but to conditions beyond the reach of policy.

Apart from the behavior of economic policy and of international influences on the price level, there are several other powerful influences at work on the long-term price behavior of all developed economies. These other causes may be described as sociological, structural, institutional changes in the economic system that contribute a structural component to the inflation rate. They are not generally amenable to policy constraint; indeed, the effort to control their consequences through conventional aggregative economic policy may have prohibitive social and economic costs.

The record of inflation in the last two decades is colored by a progressive evolution in economic institutions, and the legislated objectives of the economic system, particularly in the years between 1965 and 1980, which witnessed an elaboration of social compacts in the area of social security, medical insurance, unemployment protection, and welfare programs. This proliferating structure of nonmarket costs is referred to in chapter 1 and is further described in chapter 9. Here it should be noted that the rapid growth of these programs (and others) carries obvious significance for the underlying inflationary tendencies of the system—not simply because they run headlong through the federal budget and account for much of the deficits now being experienced, but also because they deliberately break the free-market bond between risk and reward. The third-party payment systems that prevail across much of these programs inevitably stimulate demand for services (for example, medical services), and lower some of the incentives on which crude economic efficiency rests. They are intended to reach ethical objectives, not economic ones; their cost tends to be distributed in part, by inflation.

These reflections on some of the more obvious evolving aspects of the U.S. economy (and of all modern, developed economies) would seem to be essential parts of the understanding of modern inflation; they help to disclose the limits of economic policy when it seeks to confront the inflation issue, and they help to clarify why grimly determined efforts to treat inflation through only conventional restrictive policies carry such heavy costs and frequently produce perverse results. The actual prevailing institutional and sociological structure of the system is an integral part of the real world to which economic policy must address itself; that world contains an inflation tendency that inheres in our institutions.

A target of zero inflation, espoused (perhaps very circumspectly) by the Federal Reserve, is a partly moralistic objective, like the old "balanced federal budget"; in the real world, it is equally impracticable. Today's inflation is heavily in service industries (see figure 7–3), very lightly in the goods side of the system, which is operating in a very competitive world market. Zero inflation might well require negative price change in the goods industries, a condition few businesspersons would favor.

Economists do not like this argument; evolving sociological conditions are hard to quantify, they do not seem to help in forecasting, they tend to escape from presumably scientific theories of the origins of inflation, they seem to somewhat reduce the significance of pure economics, and they suggest limits to its power to direct events. Yet that is precisely where we are. Modern inflation is not simply painted on the real world by errors of economic policy; it is in the grain. If monetary policy is to obliterate *all* evidence of inflation in the system arising from *all* the multiple causes, it will have to be violent and, periodically, extremely costly, as indeed it has been in several prolonged episodes over the past twenty years.

These reflections on inflation and its causes lead to the following con-

Figure 7–3. Measures of the Inflation Rate

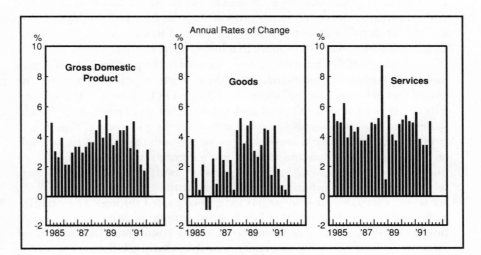

Sources: U.S. Department of Commerce; The Conference Board.

clusions, useful in appraising the future of the U.S. inflation rate and the policies that will be used to combat them:

1. Doctrinal crusades against inflation that rest on a narrow policy-oriented view of its causes cannot be successful and carry heavy potential cost. Crusading zeal on inflation should be treated circumspectly; the crusade often draws support from parochial objectives.

2. There are rates of inflation that are clearly detrimental to the system as a whole and to its future. Leaving this issue simply in the hands of the Federal Reserve is logically wrong, impractical in the real world, and occasionally dangerously costly. Conversely, there are targets for inflation rates that are unrealistically and unsustainably low; dedicating policy to such unrealistic objectives over any prolonged period carries heavy real costs. To the extent that inflation is structural and sociological, its home is in the structure of legislation and custom that dictate nonmarket objectives for the system.

3. The budget deficits that persisted in the 1980s and threaten to continue far into the 1990s are abnormally and dangerously high. They represent a major departure from the federal budget experience of the postwar years and vastly complicate the efforts of the Federal Reserve to maintain credit conditions compatible with vigorous growth of private business. Left untreated, they must, in the end, threaten to restore the struggle between monetary policy and fiscal policy that produced the interest rates and de-

plorable economic experience of mid-1981 to mid-1982. They are not compatible with a system that depends mainly on private incentive for its energy and on private investment for its growth. Indeed, losses of productive new investment during recessions induced by Federal Reserve struggles with inflation are themselves inflationary in a longer-term context.

4. Deficits of the immense size experienced in the past several years may have such complex consequences that their inflation potential may be disguised and deferred into the future. As indicated in Chapter 6, the huge deficits of the years since 1982 produced a shortage of real saving in the United States, and required a massive capital inflow for their financing. This inflow from the rest of the world inevitably passed through the market for the dollar, driving up its value and making foreign goods appear cheap. The sequential result was a rapid rise in imports of goods into the United States, which depressed the inflation rate throughout the goods sector of the U.S. economy. Inevitably, the dollar has long since passed through a speculative peak, and its immense and rapid decline, beginning in early 1985 and continuing far into 1992, is reversing some of the conditions that suppressed inflation. It is possible, but not really probable, that the inflation rate in the remainder of this decade will be moderately higher than might be implied by domestic economic conditions themselves, but any bursts of inflation beyond, let us say, a four percent annual rate will almost certainly be owing to temporary uncontrollable and unpredictable developments.

5. Since our institutional structure and the social and political commitments of our economic system play so significant a role in the inflation rate, efforts to contain this cause are fundamental to the restraint of general inflation. Progress in constraining the inflationary consequences of institutions would relieve the overcommitment of the Federal Reserve to this issue, which has led it in the past to engage in broad and costly assaults on the measured inflation rate. In pursuit of this objective, the Congress should be made intelligently aware of the fact that although transfer programs may be an essential and desirable response of a democratic political system, they are not free goods; they carry connotations of some degree of inflation, the acceptance of some degree of recession, or both. The ethical considerations that have led to the enlargement of transfer programs are valid recognitions of a need to ameliorate extremes in the distribution of income, health, education, and opportunity. Their growth, however, inevitably elevates the inflation rate associated with high employment. The benefits of these programs are in a trade-off relationship with the inefficiencies and costs associated with an elevated inflation rate.

6. Apart from the issue of the treatment of social costs, other mechanisms characteristic of mixed economies have played a role in elevating inflation. The institutions by which the trend of *wage rates* was set in the United States in the 1960s and 1970s—particularly the leapfrogging of sequential three-year wage settlements reached in the course of tough and pro-

longed struggles over shares—were clearly an inflation machine. This machine has been very largely dismantled during the period of intense pressure on American manufacturing industries from the flood of imports. There has been no leapfrogging of settlements; cost-of-living wage adjustments have been removed or modified. American labor no longer takes its lead from powerful industrial unions in traditional industries; instead, it has learned to seek stability and security in negotiating wage settlements.

7. The deterioration of *educational standards* at lower- and middle-school levels elevates the unemployment threshhold below which inflation will accelerate in the 1990s; a massive general and technological educational effort will be essential to reach satisfactory employment levels at satisfactory rates of inflation. Further extension of *protectionism* in the United States would contribute in an important way to domestic inflation; a gradual and orderly adjustment of the dollar toward a trade-determined valuation (now perhaps complete), together with intense effort to improve efficiency through direct investment, would be, in the end, much less inflationary and has many other obvious advantages over protectionism. *All* forms of *indexation*—indexation of benefits in the transfer programs, indexation of wages, even indexation of tax brackets in the personal income tax code—are proinflationary in that they compromise natural market forces that resist inflation and remove the need to confront inflation consequences directly. (In effect, they restore the issue to the Federal Reserve, which must provide the funds to finance a rise in costs and incomes.) By transmitting transient elevations of cost into permanent income flows, indexation converts cyclical or sporadic price change into general inflation.

In the end, the inflation issue in the United States will be viewed in this broadly historical, institutional context, not simply as a battleground of conflicting theories. Modern inflation is a complex social phenomenon. Broad recognition of its real roots is necessary if inflation is to be managed effectively. The prudent observer will still have to watch the price indexes and will still have to expect that a rise in the measured inflation rate will evoke the characteristic tightening of monetary conditions and the characteristic rise in interest rates that remain the conventional responses to inflation fears. And for the foreseeable future, he will have to watch the course of the dollar; significant weakness in the currency will continue to suggest some degree of imported inflation, as costs of imported materials and products rise. The dollar, the price indexes, and interest rates, taken together, comprise a central challenge to the Federal Reserve, in its pursuit of policies that will foster growth and price stability in the new internationalized markets of the 1990s.

A few last words on the shape of this issue in the 1990s. Inflation is not simply a price issue, but also an income issue. In a sense, income inflation is a more predictive component of inflation than price inflation itself. Price inflation would have little chance of persevering if it were not accompanied by income inflation, since sellers would quickly be priced out of markets under such conditions. In recent years, and prospectively for the next few years, income inflation has been almost deplorably low—too low to support recovery in demand and output, and certainly too low to support any considerable revival of price inflation. Policy is now appropriately directed much more to economic revival than to inflation control. This is clearly as it should be, given the very modest potentials for economic growth, as described in chapter 8.

Finally, we should note a large and important bridge now carrying a lot of meaningful traffic from the international subject of the last chapter to the inflation subject of this one.

The United States is now a totally integrated component of an international financial and real economy. Its capacity and its labor force compete across international borders with the entire developed world and, particularly with reference to labor force, the low-cost developing world as well. The extent of this change is not fully measured by our trade position with the rest of the world, which is not great but certainly better than it was five years ago; the world competition imposes powerful restraints on pricing throughout the goods sector and, therefore, on wages throughout the goods sector.

The change wrought by internationalization is thus from inflation to disinflation—a crucial alteration in the metabolism of the system. Efforts at cost control would seem in the first instance to provide the conditions for a considerable improvement in earnings of U.S. corporations; but when the whole goods sector is engaged in cost control at the same time, as has been the case for the past several years, the labor market suffers heavy damage, in terms both of long-term layoff and deteriorated personal income. The pressures of international disinflation on the behavior of individual economies is by no means isolated to the United States, although it is probably augmented here by the particular developments in debt formation during the 1980s. Among eleven trading countries—the United States and Canada, four countries in Europe and five in the Pacific region—every country was experiencing a substantially lower inflation rate in 1992 than prevailed during the 1980s. In only two countries—Korea and Italy—is the current rate over three percent; and only in Germany, facing most particular abnormalities, is the inflation rate higher than it was on average during the 1980s; even there it appears to be falling.

This is a disinflating world environment, in which mistakes are no longer bailed out by ensuing inflation—a consideration that has made lenders and borrowers far more cautious than normal. It has made purchasing agents far more conservative, in the absence of a threat of price rises in what they buy. It has made investors in plant and equipment more cautious, given the presence of capacity availabilities not simply at home, but throughout the developed world. And, of course, it has made consumers more cautious (witness the continuing decline in installment debt outstanding) as they struggle with an environment in which inflation no longer bails out debtors.

Inflation can be too low, as well as too high, given the social burdens requiring nominal funding throughout the developed world. The *international* inflation rate is now uncomfortably low. The condition by no means forecasts disaster, but it does argue that national economic policies for the future are going to have to focus on stimulating growth, and for a considerable period will have to forego any serious attention to the risk of inflation. That option has been earned by the intelligent, cautionary respect for inflation that has brought the rate down so far. Options to stimulate growth should be picked up with enthusiasm over the next few years, even if they suggest some moderate strengthening in the world's price and wage levels. This attitude is beginning to organize electorates everywhere, and, of course, it is infiltrating political campaigns everywhere, including the one in progress in the United States as this book goes to press.

8

The Wave of The Future

Apart from the interests of economic theorists seeking the ultimate natural laws governing the workings of an economic system, the utility of economics for us plain folks—businesspersons, consumers, even the makers of policy—lies in the insight it can shed on the future of the real world and its significance for us in the planning of our own economic behavior. In impressively opaque mathematical excursions in the economic journals, the academicians seek eternal laws; the rest of us want to know what's likely to happen. The economic history capsuled briefly in chapter 1 stopped, as all history does, at the present; the ensuing chapters sought to illuminate aspects of that history with a bearing on the future and to provide a statistical base for the construction and then the continuous maintenance of an alert understanding of the present, looking toward its significance for the future.

What, then, does the future seem to hold? If the great wave of growth emanating from the explosion at the end of World War II has been exhausted, culminating in a final speculative display of financial fireworks in the 1980s, what can be said about the environment of the 1990s? Chapter 4 documented the character of the short-term business cycle, describing it as an inevitable manifestation of a free market system. But what about the condition of the underlying trend on which the cycle rides?

As this is written in the fall of 1992, the views of probable business conditions in the 1990s vary, of course, as they always do. But almost all of them rest on a common underlying conceptual structure. That structure calls for a general continuation of satisfactory underlying growth, periodically interrupted by more or less conventional recessions. *In other words, they rest on the view that the 1990s will represent a piece of economic history seamlessly joined to the behavior of the U.S. economy in the postwar years.*

Despite the argument of chapter 1, this thesis has much going for it. In a large number of aspects, the underlying structure of the U.S. system has to be said to be a continuity. Its legal structure has not been significantly altered; the composition of demand has not changed radically; the formal powers and intentions of monetary and fiscal policy, as described in chapter 5, are unchanged. In the distribution of its assets between public and private, nothing much has happened. Its relative dependence on direct and indirect taxes is little altered. In all these broad aspects, it would be difficult to distinguish the American economy of the early 1990s from a predecessor year a quarter of a century earlier. *The burden of proof certainly rests on an argument that the underlying behavior of the U.S. economy will be different in the decade ahead from what it has been in several past decades.*

And yet the *feel* of the U.S. business situation in 1992 is different, in obvious and in subtle ways, from the historical recollection—the racial memory of economists. This is not just a matter of the atypically slow recovery from the 1990–1991 recession. Indeed, the Federal Reserve's actions in late 1991, and again in early 1992, marked a trough in cyclical pessimism. And, in any event, the 1990–1991 recession itself was unspectacular. *What is at issue is not dangers posed by the business-cycle machinery described in chapter 4, but the condition of the substructure of the U.S. system that controls its longer-term growth potential.*

The definition of a turning point in a long-term trend is bound to be uncertain, equivocal, a complex empirical proposition. An economy is not a rigid object; while its parts are interrelated, there are gross and variable leads and lags in the relationships among them. A turning point in long-term economic behavior should be expected to occur over considerable time, and the evidence of its occurrence would appear *seriatim* over years. Under such conditions, a change in underlying trend would appear first as a trivially low possibility, temporarily inseparable from business-cycle concerns (as it has been since 1989). The possibility would then rise, as evidence consistent with the hypothesis of a change in trend gradually accumulates. In the matter of identifying a change in underlying trend, economists face a typical vexation: They must observe and avoid premature conclusion as quantitative evidence accumulates toward qualitative change.

Such a progressive study must itself be guided by the selection and definition of an hypothesis. *The hypothesis offered here is that accumulating changes over the past ten years have precipitated a general change in the conditions that determine the potential growth rate of the economic system as a whole.* Areas in which such progressive change has occurred are described briefly below. The areas are suspiciously numerous; many of them interact with others in ways that may enlarge their aggregate effect. They all raise questions for lengthy study, which cannot be undertaken here. But each issue is legitimately related to the long-term trend, and each view expressed is in general consonance with the findings of good current research.

Two preparatory points. First, many of the issues raised below have been visibly present in the U.S. system for a considerable period of time—

some of them since 1989 and a few of them for as much as a decade. For most of their existence, it was possible to treat them as individual and local—subject, when we got around to it, to direct treatment. But the general deterioration in many of them seems to have accelerated over the past four or five years—ever since the crescendo of public and private debt formation in the middle of the 1980s. In the course of the past several years, the issues appear to have grown together—to have congealed—under the pressures of drawn-out weakness in the economy as a whole, so that the individual treatment of each issue has grown more difficult and less promising, as the resources available to deal with it have failed to grow apace with the dimensions of the problems themselves.

Secondly, the extended weakness of the system in the late 1980s and early 1990s reflects the presence of a kind of intermediate cycle—longer than ordinary recession but perhaps not truly secular—arising out of the huge debt burdens generated in the last half of the 1980s. A fascinating issue, on which it is still impossible to reach much of a conclusion, is when and how this debt cycle will be alleviated in time—whether its relief will reduce the size of the issues described below, permitting secular growth to resume at its historical rate, or whether the impact of the debt cycle has reinforced other weaknesses, and produced sets of limitations on growth that will survive even the ultimate restoration of better balance in the private and public debt structure. It may be a while before the two hypotheses can be separated out empirically. *And it might be noted that they are not entirely independent of each other; the deterioration in economic conditions described below doubtless has made it more difficult to restore normal debt relationships for the system as a whole.*

The Growth Rate Itself

In appraising the current trend experience underlying business cycle fluctuations, a good place to start would be the record of growth itself (see figure 8–1). The compound growth rate in the four years ended in 1986 was about four percent, the highest such four-year record since 1979. After 1986, the compound four-year growth rate subsided steadily to about 1.7 percent in 1991, and evidently about 1.2 percent in 1992 (assuming a growth rate in calendar 1992 of about two percent).

The four-year period 1988 to 1992 thus shows the lowest compound growth since the four years ending in 1983, when the compound rate was about 0.7 percent. The year-to-year movements within these two four-year periods are compared in inserts to figure 8–1. Very clearly, they are quite different; the earlier period was pronouncedly cyclical, incorporating the experience of the 1980 recession and the 1982 recession, and terminating in a

Figure 8–1. The Decline in the Longer-Term Growth Rate

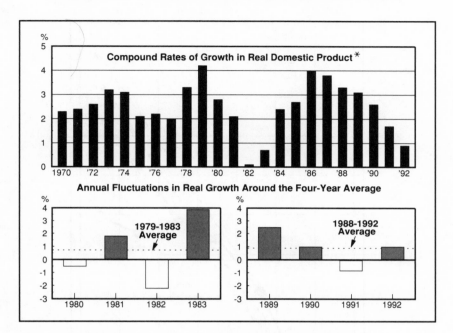

*Bars represent compound growth for four years ended in year plotted.
Sources: U.S. Department of Commerce; The Conference Board.

growth rate of about four percent in 1983. In contrast, the experience embodied in the 1992 four-year average is much less cyclical, in the sense that the average annual deviation from the mean is only about half that experienced in the earlier period. *It is fair to say that the only other recent period in which the four-year growth rate was so low was primarily a cyclical phenomenon, whereas in the current period the experience seems much more readily characterized as a subsidence of underlying growth, only modestly affected by the cycle.* In fact, the distinguishing feature of the recession incorporated in the later period is not striking cyclical weakness; as recessions go, it would have to be classified as relatively mild. Its seriousness, even now, almost two years after it began, lies in the sense of underlying structural weaknesses that seem to limit cyclical recovery, even though the prerequisites for cyclical recovery have been in place for several quarters.

It is a striking fact about recent economic performance that U.S. output falls below virtually any trend value constructed from U.S. experience since 1960 (see figure 8–2). If the growth rate of real output were to be two percent in 1992, and three percent in 1993, the four-year growth rate for 1989

Figure 8–2. Real Output Measured Against Trend Values

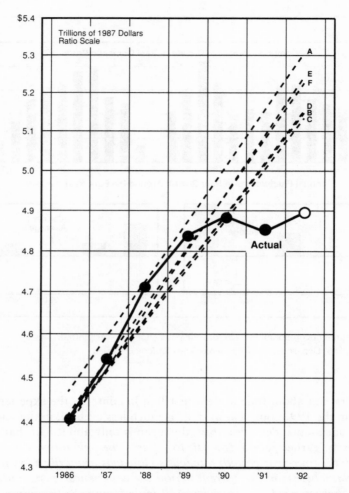

Note: Fitted logarithmic trends: A = 1960 to 1990; B = 1965 to 1990; C = 1970 to 1990; D = 1975 to 1990; E = 1980 to 1990; F = 1985 to 1990.

Sources: U.S. Department of Commerce; The Conference Board.

to 1993 would still be only 1.3 percent—about half of what is often taken to be the sustainable long-term trend.

The Trend in the Labor Force

Statistically and conceptually, the potential growth rate is considered to be a function of the growth rate of the labor force and the presumed improvement in productivity. In an elementary arithmetical sense, growth is a product of the number of people available for work, and the output achieved per person. This is a pretty simple dissection of the growth process, full of obvious unspecified assumptions. But as a crude first pass at the growth potential of the United States in recent years, projectible into the future, it requires some treatment. Figures 8–3 and 8–4 portray the twenty-year behavior of variables related to the future supply of labor. For both the civilian labor force and nonfarm employment, trends have been fitted to the history of the past twenty years and projected out into the future. The results say something interesting and not terribly comforting about what the future may hold for output relative to past experience. In particular, the civilian labor force has been falling, relative to trend, for many years; experience in 1992 seems to have continued the relative downtrend. Participation rates for both males and females have flattened out. In 1991, the actual labor force fell almost six million people short of the level that would have prevailed if the 1970–1990 trend had been maintained. The cyclical rise in the unemployment rate in the

Figure 8–3. Labor Force Participation Rate and the Nonfarm Employment Shortfall

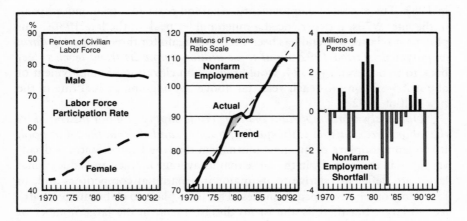

Sources: U.S. Department of Labor; The Conference Board.

Figure 8–4. Unemployment and the Labor Force Shortfall

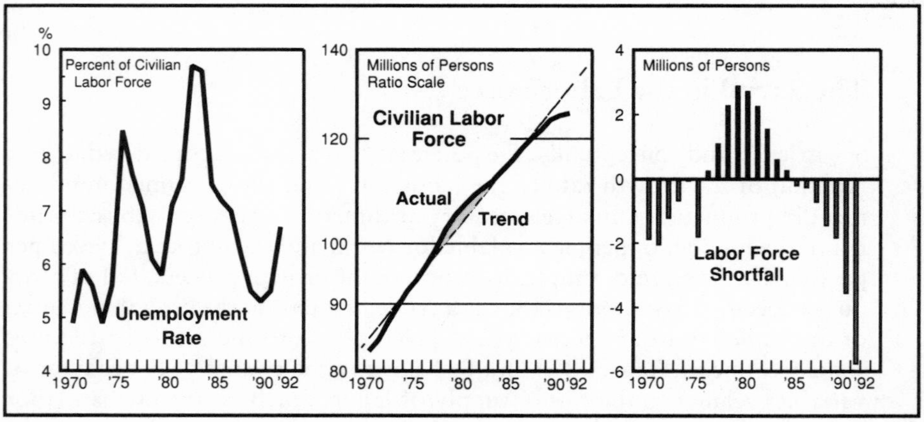

Sources: U.S. Department of Labor; The Conference Board.

early 1990s was moderate, partly because of the slowing growth of the labor force. If the labor force had continued to grow at its trend rate and job creation were to have proceeded at its actual rate, the unemployment rate, near its peak in early 1992, would have been close to ten percent—a far more severe result than could have been attributed to the mild cyclical experience of 1990–1991.

At least until 1990, the *employment* experience stuck much more closely to the twenty-year trend; in fact, it hugged it with the exception of the intense cyclical experience surrounding the 1981–1982 recession. But in 1991, actual employment departed sharply from trend—about as sharply as it did in 1982. The excess of employment over trend reached a pronounced peak in the late 1970s; it experienced a much milder peak in the late 1980s; employment relative to trend has been declining again for three years. *Nonfarm employment started 1992 about three million below its trend level*; to get back to trend, even by 1994, would require an elevation of employment of about 2.3 million jobs each year, far above the ongoing annual rate in the first half of 1992.

Obviously more important than the crude supply of labor measured by the labor force statistics is the quality, training, and skills in the labor pool. It is a commonplace of business journalism that the United States is disadvantaged in this respect, in the sense that its average literacy and educational levels are deficient relative to its major international competitors and, in fact, most other developed countries. This is no place to elaborate on a subject so large, but there is almost no disagreement, in the large number of studies of this crucial issue that have appeared in the past few years, that new entrants into the U.S. labor force are poorly equipped to undertake the increasingly technical jobs that are rapidly replacing low-level clerical and physical jobs. (Among those with less than twelve years' schooling, the unemployment rate is about twelve percent, even now.) *According to the Bureau of Labor Statistics' projections of employment skills levels, there will be virtually zero growth in unskilled job categories in the 1990s.* As so many studies put it, the United States faces a serious mismatch between available skills and available jobs—an obvious threat to productivity performance.

The Productivity Outlook

With respect to productivity itself—the other variable in the growth equation—the statistics again suggest some degree of caution beyond the issue of skills mismatch. Studies of the U.S. investment and saving rate over the past ten years have varied significantly in their findings. But some of the most careful recent studies support the view that the U.S. structure, as it appears early in the decade of the 1990s, remains heavily consumptionoriented; its saving rate and its aggregate investment rate are significantly lower than those of its international competitors. Pessimism on this subject can perhaps go too far; a substantial improvement in productivity has been occurring in manufacturing industries, even under conditions of stable or falling volume, and even in the presence of a low aggregate saving rate and a very large diversion of investment funds into financing the budget deficit.

Nevertheless, recent studies continue to reveal a low aggregate saving propensity and a lower aggregate investment propensity than appears among our industrial competitors. The U.S. national saving rate appears to have fallen significantly, even after standardization for changing age and income levels.

Given the mix of economic activity now characteristic of the United States, it can be expected that productivity gain can maintain its recent levels, but any possible acceleration would be unlikely to make up a significant portion of the loss of output potential attributable to the slower growth and strained skill distribution of the labor force.

This should be called a soft conclusion. In the presence of slow growth in the labor force, capital investment may actually be encouraged. In manufacturing, productivity gain in the United States from 1989 to 1991 was generally good (although less than half of the gain in Germany and about forty percent of the gain in Japan). But the inclusion of service industries in the aggregate productivity measure produces deplorable total performance—a trend rate of 1.1 percent since 1984 and zero net change from 1988 to 1991.

The saving and investment expansions required to elevate this performance are not by any means discernible yet.

A Laboring Government

The government sector in the United States in the early 1990s demands special consideration with respect to its bearing on the growth potential. It might be said of government as a whole that it has temporarily exhausted its capacity to provide the steady, and now and then substantial, energy to the private sector that it has offered virtually throughout the postwar years. The budget deficits confronting the system stand in the way not just of providing much cyclical stimulus now, but of maintaining normal secular growth in governmental demand.

At the same time, the effective functioning of government at all levels is now handicapped by high levels of policy uncertainty, traceable to a lack of clear convictions on its theoretical position and on its proper role; by heavy and growing entitlement and transfer requirements; by public attitudes that demand services without taxation; and by deterioration in the ethical reputation of the governors themselves. (This is not the only ethical and social problem confronting the United States in the 1990s; others are appraised below.)

The Economic Impasse

At the federal level, an immense budget deficit is now in place, and it is likely to continue for several years (see figure 8–5). In the main, the deficit reflects an enormous and still growing volume of transfers and insurance-type claims that provide little economic stimulus but, nevertheless, absorb revenues and require financing. The expenditures of the federal government on payroll and goods, which provide direct stimulus to national output, are dwarfed by the transfers, and real outlay is likely to shrink further in the course of the ongoing decline in defense spending. While it is economically "wasteful" in that it contributes little directly to the nation's industrial base on which productivity performance rests, defense spending is a large industry, and the armed forces are a large employer. The real and anticipated curtailment of the defense budget has already precipitated decline in the industry, and further decline certainly lies ahead. Unequivocally beneficial in the long run, the curtailment is bound to produce dislocations and adjustments throughout the defense sector for many years ahead.

The opportunities to convert this decline in outlay into a stimulative decline in taxes are obstructed by the size of the aggregate deficit and by the continuing uptrend in transfer-type outlay. The prospect of low inflation and the indexation of personal tax brackets tend to limit the growth of fed-

Figure 8–5. The Swollen Federal Deficit

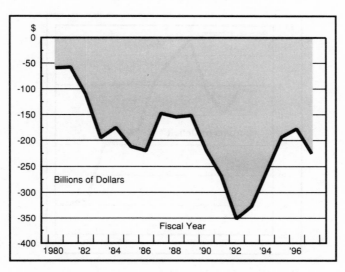

Note: Years 1992 to 1997 are Congressional Budget Office estimates.
Sources: Department of the Treasury; Congressional Budget Office; The
Conference Board.

eral funds. Demands for the further extension of social programs—made
more urgent by the effects of a four-year slowdown in growth, employment,
and incomes in the private sector and by the evidence provided by the Los
Angeles riots in the spring of 1992—seem very likely to rule out any stimulative increase of direct outlay.

Comment on the limitations confronting the federal government must
be applied with equal force to the condition of state and local governments,
whose aggregate employment is five times that of the federal government
and whose demands approximate eleven percent of all output. After a four-
year deterioration, the budgets of state and local governments in 1991, including their unfunded social insurance costs, are now in deficit by about
forty billion dollars (see figure 8–6). About thirty states are in deficit in
1992; a further rise is expected in 1993. Nearly twenty states are eliminating
programs; fourteen are engaged in layoffs. (But supplemental appropriations
for Aid to Families with Dependent Children are occurring in nineteen
states, and eighteen are increasing Medicaid outlays.) A number of cities and
counties confront the same conditions. Instead of providing their customary
long-term noncyclical stimulus, the state and local governments must be expected to be in a period of consolidation for the next half decade—a period
of absorption of energy rather than creation of energy—as they restrain their
rate of outlays and maintain or increase their tax revenues and user charges.

With respect to the role of government within the system, the decade of

Figure 8–6. The Descent of State and Local Budgets

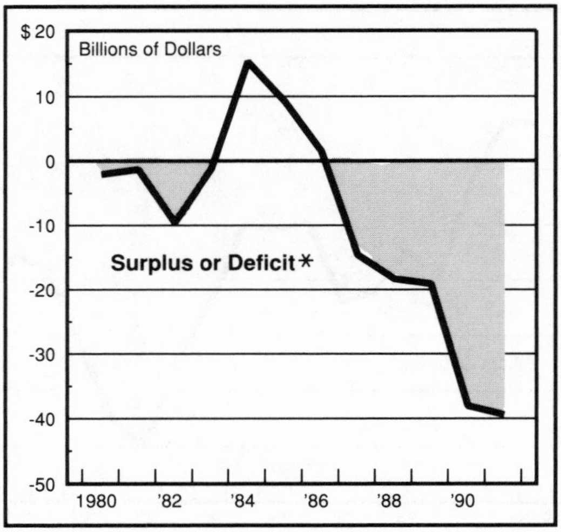

*Including unfunded Social Security costs.
Sources: U.S. Department of Commerce; The Conference Board.

the 1990s has thus begun under conditions profoundly different from those prevailing in preceding decades—even, in a broad sense, in the entire postwar period. At no time in the postwar period, for example, has it ever been true that about two-thirds of the state governments and a substantial percentage of local governments, including many major cities, are confronting budget dilemmas that seem to call for contractionary behavior, at the same time that the federal budget is running an immense structural deficit. Somewhere up ahead, the restraint and rationalization of the government sector that may be the ultimate outcome of the pressures on its finances will free margins of resources to be used in increased public investment and with greater efficiency (that is, with greater value added) in the private sector. But that would appear to be a hopeful prospect for more distant years of the decade; for now, the constraints on government seem to impose a limitation on the energy of the system as a whole, and on its prospects for growth.

The Political Impasse

The problems of government in making a contribution to orderly growth and in the provision of a suitable environment for private industry in the United States are not limited to their simple budgetary constraints. All government units in the United States, but certainly most particularly the federal government, are now subjected to intense pressure from single-issue constituencies, and from more general constituencies seeking favorable treatment in tax and spending legislation. These pressures are familiar enough here and elsewhere, but their intensity has grown as the U.S. growth rate has subsided, enhancing a host of social and distributional problems that had been present in any event for decades.

In the presence of prolonged sluggish growth, the kinds of social issues to which government addresses itself have congealed into a tough, hard-shelled mass that seemingly demands legislative treatment because free markets themselves are unable to provide solutions in anything approaching the improbable time frame sought by the electorate. Slow growth in real income over a prolonged period, combined with widespread publicity that policies followed in the 1980s shifted the income distribution to the right (which indeed they did), have acted to generate a loose and rather implausible definition of a "middle class" that has been disadvantaged for a decade and merits favorable tax consideration; while below that class in the income distribution is now an "underclass," seemingly still more urgently in need of governmental assistance.

The still inchoate state of the debate on health insurance in the United States, and continuing negative information on the quality of education available in the United States, are perhaps the largest issues confronting government and the electorate. But the tendency of voters to place very high priorities on such programs, as well as on drugs and crime, is not now matched by their willingness to finance increased participation of government efforts in these areas, and the political leadership (as well as the money) required to face up to the costs realistically still seems to have been lacking thus far in 1992.

All of these issues are made still more difficult by what appears to be a considerable decline in the public reputation of government itself and of the politicians who manage it. *As the issues have grown, poll after poll reveals a rising sense of public urgency—even a desire for a more active role for government; but the actual trust available to politicians to deal with them fairly and effectively seems diminished.* The weakened political posture of government disposes it toward politically inspired concessions that are not in the interest of long-run growth. *More than at any time in recent memory, a government struggling with its own reputation confronts large socioeconomic issues made larger by the absence of the kind of vigorous growth that would restrain the problems and provide increments of resources to address them.*

The United States in the World: An Emerging Normal

Some brief identification of the figures and trends in the U.S. international situation was offered in chapter 6. Some of those materials are restated here, with particular reference to their bearing on the U.S. growth rate ahead.

Two decades ago, the United States was a relatively small participant in world markets. Throughout the postwar years, until 1971, it ran modest surpluses in its merchandise account and in its balance on goods and services. For twenty-five years after World War II, the U.S. economy was almost totally self-contained, unthreatened internationally, and full of options to behave as it wished.

In 1992, it is a much larger participant in the world market, in the simple arithmetical sense that its aggregate trade with the rest of the world, relative to its own output, has very nearly doubled, while foreign holdings of U.S. real and financial assets have grown even faster. The U.S. international relationship has given way to circumstances in which its markets and suppliers are now strikingly integrated with a global economy, while our global competitors have become much larger, much more efficient, much better equipped with competitive technological capacities.

This is a new world to the U.S. economy, now only recently accessible to long-term study and projection. In the 1970s and the 1980s, the initial stages of this transition were disguised and contorted by the collapse of the gold-exchange standard, the rapid transition into floating rates, the explosions of oil prices, and the Reagan fiscal and monetary policies of the early 1980s. As indicated in chapter 6, the consequences of those policies were to drive the dollar upward in an unprecedented crescendo, making U.S. products extremely expensive overseas and precipitating a flood of imports of relatively high technological character, as distinguished from the high-labor content goods that had traditionally dominated our imports. The subsequent decline of the dollar in the last half of the 1980s, as dramatic as its earlier rise, eliminated the exchange-rate *cause* of the growth of importation and sent exports on a course of dramatic expansion. But the consequences of the history of the 1980s have remained firmly in place; our principal competitors, particularly Germany and Japan (and now a number of formidable competitors in the Far East other than Japan) have consolidated the footholds and market positions gained earlier in the 1980s.

The United States runs a continuing, although now shrunken, deficit in its merchandise trade with the rest of the world. In recent years, the deficit has been reduced quite considerably, as the current recession and the years of slow growth that preceded it curtailed imports, while exports expanded sharply, partly because of relatively fast growth of markets among our trading partners and partly because of quite successful competitive readjustments in American manufacturing industry.

The United States entered 1992 with a trade deficit lower than it has experienced in a decade. The goods industries have achieved a substantial adjustment to the global economy. But the new "normal" is likely to settle into a tough competitive environment, in which growth of exports even faintly resembling the doubling of export volume between 1986 and 1991 is not at all probable. The U.S. growth rate now has an international exposure.

Many of our trading partners are no longer growing rapidly themselves. In the presence of renewed growth at home, a "leakage" of cyclical energy, in the direction of our trading partners, now has to be expected; it actually appeared in the spring of 1992. Even modest resumption of growth in 1992 is acting to elevate imports, while slowed growth and even actual recession among our trading partners has suppressed exports.

What should be concluded about this new international world in which the United States participates is not that the participation in a global economy is necessarily damaging, but simply that it forecloses the large abnormal options formerly open to the system to pursue its own independent course without regard to demand and technological conditions in the rest of the world. *While we need not fear the devastations suffered in the wake of the abnormal dollar in the first half of the 1980s, neither should we count on a replay of the resurgence of exports, as the dollar fell in the last half of the 1980s. The new "normal" is a tough competitive environment.*

Private-Sector Considerations

With respect to the great bulk of private demand in the U.S. economic system, there are some limitations to growth in the 1990s. These limitations do not argue for important impairment of the trend of private sector activities; but they do carry a suggestion that no more than moderate gains should be expected in these markets for several years. In general, the concerns here partly reflect the fact that the debt and asset explosion of the 1980s, culminating in the slow growth of 1988 to 1990, the recession of 1990–1991, and the halting resumption of growth in 1992, precipitated immense excesses in the U.S. balance sheet, more serious and harder to relieve than the ordinary excesses of ordinary recession.

A first consideration is the relatively low level of household formation that is expected to prevail during the 1990s—a consideration parallel to the low labor-force growth rate described above. The Bureau of Labor Statistics' so-called "moderate" assumption for household formation in the 1990s is for less than half of the average rate in the years 1975 to 1990. Household formation is a significant, although by no means determining, element in the aggregate demand for residential building, household goods, and automobiles. The impact of the household-formation rate on these markets has to be taken in conjunction with such other determinants of demand as the level of private debt; the debt service burden related to income; the availability of incremental credit; and the real interest rates on which credit is available.

The debt burden issue bears, of course, on debt-related markets: the housing market, the market for consumer durables, and the business market for plant and equipment. The awesome debt cycle introduced into U.S. economic performance by the extraordinary growth of debt in the 1980s hardly requires additional comment here. Suffice it that the private sector entered the 1990s with unprecedented relationships of debt to income in both the personal sector and the corporate sector. In reaction to these levels, the rate of net increase in debt formation slowed dramatically in 1990 and still further in 1991 (see figure 8–7). It has not revived significantly even in 1992. Escape from the consequences of the debt burden acquired in the 1980s has to be expected to be prolonged for a strong logical reason: The curtailment of new debt formation, which is the general (and least painful) way by which a debt excess can be absorbed, itself suppresses economic activity and hence the incomes available to service the debt. The comforts of vigorous growth are thus denied to the process of debt restructuring, tending to extend it and make it more painful. This unhappy piece of debt-cycle machinery doubtless helps to explain the failure of economic recovery to have gotten well started in 1991 and 1992.

Finally, the real interest rates in the United States remain abnormally high. While the nominal rates have fallen quite substantially, particularly at the short end of the yield curve, inflation has fallen away sharply, and *expectations* of inflation (really the operable variable with respect to the real interest rate) have also dwindled. Figure 8–8 charts a hypothetical real interest rate for short-term securities; the real rate on longer-term borrowings is much more dramatically high. The level of the real interest rate is a substantial consideration with respect to housing demand and inventory demand.

Figure 8–7. Subsiding Debt Formation: The Diminishing Stimulus

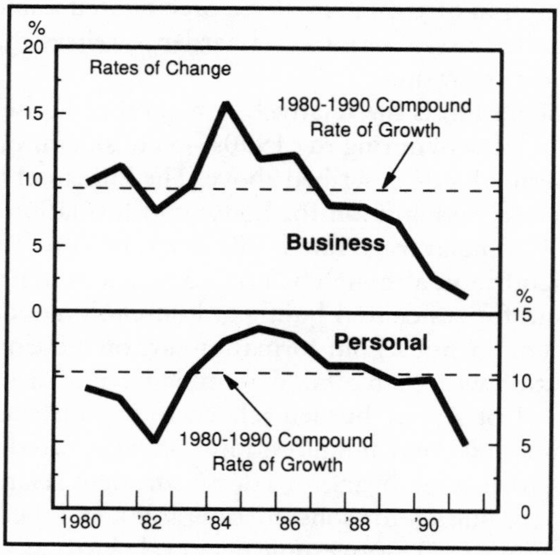

Sources: Federal Reserve; The Conference Board.

Figure 8–8. The Real Interest Rate

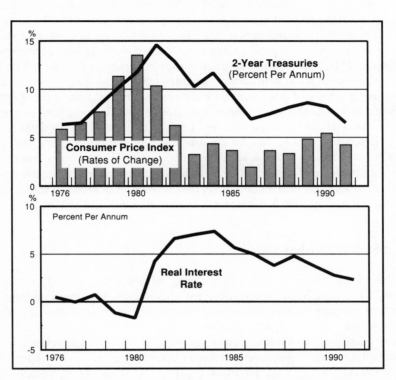

Sources: U.S. Department of Labor; Department of the Treasury; The Conference Board.

With respect to housing, the real rate is now extraordinarily high; while the mortgage rate has fallen several hundred basis points, the rate of price appreciation in the residential housing market has fallen several times that much—a fact that accounts for the modest response, thus far, of home sales and home construction in the presence of so rapid a decline in rates.

The real interest rate is also a matter given great consideration by purchasing managers, who are naturally disinclined to accumulate stocks, when the carrying costs are still considerably above their own appraisal of the potential for price appreciation of the materials they buy. The appearance of price strength in the industrial sector, when it arrives (it has not begun at all in 1992), should be considered a welcome development, since it would restore the incentive to hold and accumulate inventory.

Over the last year or so, consumer attitudes have been altered by the experience of drawn-out subsidence in the general economy and in real earnings in the presence of acute uncertainty in the labor market. Even though surveys of consumer attitudes may have clearly stabilized in 1992, the spending propensities of households seem to have entered on a slow sea-change, relative to attitudes that prevailed throughout much of the 1980s. Advertising professionals, as well as retailers and manufacturers of consumer goods, have for two years reported an apparent change in the propensity to spend, accompanied by greatly increased attention to price and quality. Much of the behavior of these attitudinal variables can be charged to the residual short-term effects of poor general business conditions. But some of it may reflect a more durable alteration in spending propensities—a kind of persisting reaction to the immense debt-and-consumption wave of the 1980s.

These observations on the condition of consumption spending in the 1990s are certainly inconclusive. But in conjunction with other troubles of the long-term trend described in this chapter, they carry a mild and uncertain corroboration of the conclusion that growth in demand in much of the 1990s will not approach the rate achieved in much of the 1980s.

The Social Burden

In the 1990s, the U.S. economy is living with a rising burden of "social costs." The conditions responsible for these costs have been present for much of the past decade and, in many instances, for several decades. Many of them are widely accepted as natural, inevitable, and even desirable programs of mixed economies; they are present, in various assortments, in virtually all developed democratic systems. But many of them are responses to visible social strains that are more pronounced in the United States than among other developed nations. The particular conditions of low growth over the past several years have tended to amplify these abnormal costs and to establish connections among them that reinforce their significance as a group. The burden of dealing with them continues to grow and spread, while the public resources and the ethical commitment (see below) required to address them have been heavily strained.

The Social Security Administration annually tabulates an all-inclusive accounting of "social welfare expenditures" under public programs. The total rate of such spending is now about one trillion dollars and rising at fifty billion dollars a year. Of this total, the federal government bears about sixty percent and the state and local governments about forty percent of the costs. Most but not all of the costs (education is the big exception) represent transfers.

The aggregate tabulation is far too broad to be analytically useful; it mixes conventional entitlements with outlays directed specifically toward troubled parts of the system; thus, it includes all social insurance, all public aid, all health and medical programs, veterans' programs, educational outlay, and housing outlay. Within the total, the federal budget incorporates about $130 billion of so-called means-tested programs—mainly Medicaid, food stamps, supplemental security income, aid to families with dependent children (AFDC), and other public welfare.

Other costs confronting the system are not so readily measurable, and what measures there are suffer from almost certain undercoverage of the direct costs and no coverage at all of the foregone output of individuals responsible for the costs. All that is available in these areas are scatter-shot statistical probes. While they are utterly undependable, they loosely confirm a widely accepted notion that an "underclass" has grown in the course of the slowing of the U.S. growth rate over the past few years—an undereducated, ill-housed, dependent, largely untaxed population, with limited access to health care, and prone to drug and alcohol addiction and crime—a social class detached from the mainstream of the U.S. system. The burden of the direct and indirect costs of this population must certainly be substantial—and considerably in excess, even relatively, of those experienced in other developed economies, where family structure has been stronger and the issues of education, income, drugs, and crime are not so agonizingly compounded by the growth of disadvantaged racial minorities.

This disconnected and unproductive residue of the system would, by almost anyone's analytical system, place a heavy burden on the private sector and on its growth potential. Difficult to describe, difficult to measure, difficult to treat, its absorption of resources stands in the way of the vigorous real economic growth—in jobs, in incomes, in tax revenues—that would provide the incremental resources for its treatment. What anecdotal evidence (in the absence of real evidence) is available suggests that measures taken to deal with this thorny issue—often dedicated, determined, expensive, but also often divisive—have not provided anything resembling progress. In the view of some recent research, they have made it worse.

It is simply foolish not to recognize that these issues, taken together, pose a great American dilemma. Failure to treat them will perpetuate them as a dangerous and unpredictable limit to growth. But aggressive treatment of them would cost a vast multiple of what the American political process, in the presence of huge federal deficits, growing fiscal problems at state and local levels, urgent demands for middle-income tax relief, and lack of any consensus on methods, now seems at all likely to deliver. The Los Angeles riots of the spring of 1992 shed a baleful light on these issues.

The Ethical Burden

The issue posed by these social costs has been made more intractable by the ethical developments of the 1980s. That decade represented a great celebration of self-interest, unparalleled, it might be said, since a broadly similar celebration in the 1920s (which rested on the same extreme *laissez-faire* economics). Few economists, and certainly not this one, would be inclined to denigrate the usefulness of self-interest in the management of a private economy; the developments of the past several years in Eastern Europe provide all the evidence to demonstrate the agony that ultimately ensues when central command vacates market machinery. But market economies are part of a broader socioeconomic system, and it is possible to exalt self-interest to a point where it diverts attention and, of course, resources, from aggregate needs of the system.

The ethical issue here is *not* the American "work ethic," so denigrated by Japanese politicians and businesspersons. Despite all the rhetoric, the U.S. work ethic among those integrated into the ongoing work force seems in the main entirely reputable and appropriate for a society that seeks "the pursuit of happiness" defined more broadly than material standards. On the whole, Americans submit to the discipline of the marketplace, sometimes with nearly heroic patience. So do U.S. corporations, which live on the whole peaceably, if occasionally irritably, with some of the most vigorous market competition observable anywhere in the world.

The issue here is not a "work ethic," or a "business ethic" but Ethics capitalized—the "public ethic" that concerns the behavior of individuals in relation to the groups and governmental entities of which they are a part—the duties they accept in return for the rights and privileges they receive as members.

All economic systems require some ordered subordination of individual purpose to public objectives. To achieve this, they require a public ethic—widely accepted ethical practices and standards—if they are to maintain a structure suitable for long-term growth. The U.S. economy, as all free-market economies, rests on and draws coherence from an ethical structure—largely extralegal rules of conduct that preserve social order (and reduce the cost of maintaining order), provide a basis for disinterested behavior, and support respect for public authority and the rule of law itself. *An ethical system in good working order is an essential conserver of economic energy. Its deterioration carries heavy costs for the productive part of the system, in elevated security requirements; legal, advisory, and litigation costs; environmental costs; and the costs of crime, ranging all the way from pilferage to financial, managerial, and public fraud (witness the costs of the savings-and-loan disaster). Deterioration of ethics in public service generates cynical disregard for law, including tax law; it thus stimulates growth of garden-variety tax evasion and, of course, the growth of the underground economy, which was doubtless stimulated, in any event, by the increase in the numbers of discouraged workers and part-time employment over the past two years.*

The erosion of family structures multiplies educational costs, crime costs, drug costs. The decline of "disinterested" attitudes compromises the system's ability to attend to such public needs as infrastructure, adding to transportation costs and waste disposal costs ("Not in My Backyard"). It encourages the "free ride," in which those who do not conform to ethical responsibilities actually benefit from the conformance of others. The intense search for individual protection against risk, *regardless of the social costs,* drives environmental and product-liability regulation to extremes and vastly multiplies medical costs, including the cost of malpractice insurance. Relaxations of a public ethic compromise support for public programs that deal with equal opportunity, education, early family environment. Politicians themselves are skilled at sensing the diminishing of public purpose in an age of aggressive self-interest; the deteriorated public ethic often makes it mark in open appeals to interest groups—promises of programs that may well be damaging to long-term growth, but are hard to resist in the presence of an electorate trained to self-interest and unashamed to express it explicitly at the polls.

All of these conditions are, of course, always present to some degree, human beings being human; the United States is hardly alone in facing them. But they have appeared to be far more than normally present in the late 1980s and early 1990s, after a decade during which public responsibilities were so subordinated (even by, in fact particularly by, economic theorists) to the search for personal success in private markets. It may be that of all the reasons for expecting slow real growth for several years ahead, these concerns, whose connection to economic growth itself defies the methods of economics, may turn out to be among the most important. While these interests seem distant from the ordinary materials of economics, concern over them has grown among sophisticated economists and sociologists, who recognize the dependence of the economic system on a viable social and ethical structure, in which individuals accept responsibility to the totality.

This is the lee side of a cultural wave; there are signs that it is turning now, in a long reversion toward an American normal. The Los Angeles riots, the continuing reports on the condition of inner cities, deplorable statistics on U.S. educational outcomes, mounting criticism of medical services, particularly for the poor, and agonizing evidence of the growth of public and private consumption in an era of uninhibited self-interest are drawing the U.S. toward new options, both public and private, on both ethical and economic grounds. Such a reversion toward a rehabilitated public ethic would be a hopeful sign of more rational economic governance and, hence, of better economic performance.

Conclusions

This review of selected conditions affecting prospects for growth over the next several years has focused on aspects of the U.S. situation that present obstacles to achieving sustained long-term vigor. There are, of course, other and better things to say. The U.S. economy is, as it has been for decades,

Figure 8–9. Critical Trends Into the Nineties

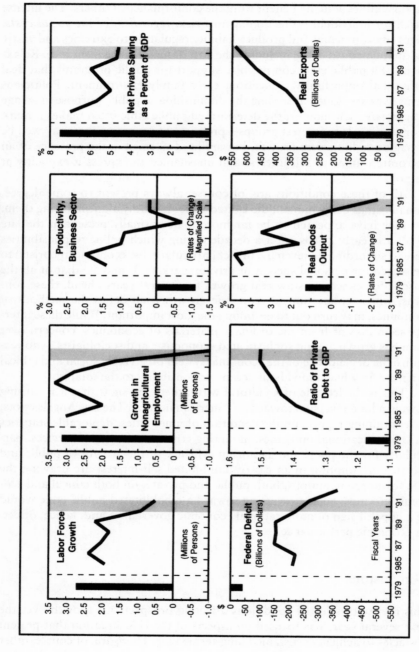

Sources: U.S. Department of Labor; U.S. Department of Commerce; Department of the Treasury; Office of Management and Budget; The Conference Board.

180

resilient and mobile with respect to both its labor force and its physical investment—probably more so than most of its competitors. It has immense material resources; its land-to-population ratio is a large multiple of the ratio that prevails among most of our industrialized competitors. It has achieved a substantial and inevitable adjustment to the globalization of real and financial markets, an adjustment that has yielded, for many parts of the system, increased competitive vigor. The gradually tightening cost controls resulting from slow growth, low earnings, and heavy interest costs, have begun to pay off as growth has resumed. Its wage-making institutions no longer threaten the system with a wage-price spiral. The likelihood of descent into deep recession or depression is too low to require comment.

All the issues raised in this chapter can be condensed into three major descriptions of the drain on long-term growth. First, the system is emerging from, but continues to be dominated by, a hangover of its "bubble-economy" characteristic of the 1980s. Figure 8–9, which summarizes the descent of economic energy in the system in the late 1980s and early 1990s, reveals the weakened condition confronting the system now. Conditions associated with this one prominent cause can be thought of as a long cycle, from which the system is now withdrawing, and may indeed overcome this group of obstacles as it continues to adjust to excessive debt and excessive supply of long-lived assets over the next two years. Profound and tough, the issues are not truly long term, and they may well taper off, slowly at first and then more rapidly, toward the middle 1990s.

Secondly, and much more truly long term, the consumption orientation of the U.S. system and its great budgetary dilemma continue to dictate inappropriate decisions with respect to taxes; for example, proposed reductions in personal taxes, the failure to increase oil taxes, the failure to legislate value-added taxes, and the failure to finance a considerably higher level of public and private investment in education, in more equal youth opportunity, and in real productive facilities, when the need is clearly accumulating.

Finally, social and ethical issues described here and their effects on the political process are deep seated and long term. The costs of a deteriorated public ethic are impossible to measure but very high with respect both to our own past record and to the current records of our competitors. *As the world's largest multiracial, multiethnic, multiclass society, the United States requires a degree of leadership as great as any nation in the world; it will take very high leadership indeed to rebuild a public ethic consistent with rapid and sustained long-term economic growth.*

9

Epilogue: A Footnote
on the Mixed Economy

The awesome outpouring of numbers describing U.S. economic conditions is a stream of evidence. It bears on behavior, not on the structure of the system or, more philosophically, its nature. Nor do the figures say anything—directly, at least—about developing *changes* in the nature of the system. The flow of evidence on the direction of economic activity, and the tendency of economists to seek guides to the future from developments in comparable periods of the past, often suffer from a lack of awareness that the U.S. economy is a living, evolving structure, with laws of motion that derive mainly from forces much broader than can be captured in ordinary economic data. Understanding the future, it might be said, is too important to be left just to economists. Long statistical series, often running back decades, are really the tracks of an evolving animal; the relevance of the early segments of such data to the present and the future deteriorates with time. No review and study of the statistical stream is thus really complete, or really in proper perspective, absent an awareness of the forces that drive the structure of the economy and what they portend for the future.

The bulk of economics operates on a paradigm of pure, free markets, in which purely self-interested individuals endlessly pursue their own advantage, under conditions of scarcity that pit one individual against another. If the world were really like this, then the gorgeous edifice of economic theory that is taught in graduate schools—and endlessly elaborated in the professional journals—would provide as good a description of economic events as physics provides for physical events, and economic predictions would be as valid as the predictions of physical scientists. *It ain't necessarily so, of course; in fact, it necessarily ain't so.*

There are individual markets in economics that are very close to perfectly free. Even for these markets—in fact, particularly for these markets—the predictive record leaves a great deal to be desired. At any point in time, superbly trained specialists in pure markets will hold very different opinions about the future.

182

The scientific base of economics thus does not work very well even where conditions are conducive to its success. Beyond such narrow markets, however, looking at large aggregative chunks of the system or at the system as a whole, the paradigm of the free market fits the real world only very loosely—and more and more loosely over time. The real world is no longer composed solely of free markets freely interacting with each other. The United States, and indeed all major Western economies, contain large and growing nonmarket structures deliberately implanted in the system to achieve objectives that a free market will not reach, or will not reach within a desired time span. Their presence in the system reflects goals, objectives, priorities that arise out of essentially political and ethical rather than economic considerations.

Such a structure—a mixture of economic, political, social, cultural, and ethical structures—is called a **mixed economy.** The description of such a system and its probable future course simply cannot be found in economic theory alone; large parts of it lie in the body of legislation mandating certain kinds of activity in the federal revenue legislation providing the funds, in the scores of government agencies regulating the limits of competitive behavior across broad sectors of the system, and, ultimately, in the public ethic that critiques and qualifies purely market outcomes.

The size and significance of these intrusions into the classical free market of economics are matters of heated political debate. The extreme positions range from warnings that increasing "socialization" is strangling the marketplace, and even threatening personal liberty, to the argument that they are hopelessly inadequate to protect ordinary citizens from exploitation by the market, and unable to protect them against the savaging of the environment by uncontrolled exploitation of technology. Not much can be learned from such heated political debate, but it is important, in appraising any longer-term future of the economy, to understand the real and durable roots of intervention.

An obvious first source and inspiration for intervention by public authorities into the marketplace is the political power conferred on an issue-oriented component of the electorate by a democratic political system. Labor, business, farmers, exporters, importers, the elderly, even the ordinary individuals struggling with the cost of living—all constitute constituencies that can bring their voting power to bear on a Congress and an administration. The much maligned bureaucracies that operate government become themselves a constituency for the development or continuation of interventions in partial disregard of the public consequences. Selective groups of taxpayers that may cut across all other constituencies can be organized to support or oppose proposed alterations in the tax code. Home builders and home buyers often unite to seek greater accommodation in housing finance; management and labor in individual industries unite to pursue protection against imports.

This source, which might be called parochial intervention in the service of individual self-interest, doubtless accounts for much of the aggregate intrusion into the marketplace. It is a big mistake, however, to assume that this is all there is to the imperfections of our markets—a mistake because it suggests that the degree of intervention can be substantially reduced by a determined Congress and a determined administration. Some of the most important interventions carry the general support of the electorate as a whole and conform to sensible economic prescriptions; others reflect deeply rooted ethical positions. The budget deficits of recent years—incurred by a Republican administration in total defiance of its own orthodoxy—testify to the deep sociological and ethical supports available to precisely those large federal programs that are mainly responsible for the deficit.

Most of the wave of interventions that came in the wake of the desperate depression years of the 1930s are now generally accepted and beyond contention. They were intended to help stabilize an economic system, to forestall the destruction wrought by deep and prolonged recession. The regulation of securities markets; the insurance provided by the Federal Deposit Insurance Corporation and the Federal Home Loan Bank Board (called the Office of Thrift Supervision as of mid-1989); the centralization of credit control in the hands of a national central bank; the progressive personal income tax; the antitrust laws; the supervision provided by the Food and Drug Administration, the Securities and Exchange Commission, the Federal Trade Commission, the Civil Aeronautics Board, and, more recently, the Environmental Protection Agency—to list only a few of the better known agencies—are in dispute only with respect to detail, not with respect to function. The grants of power to such agencies represent a broad public interest in reducing the instability the public learned to associate with the free market in the experience of the 1930s and to provide a protection against the impacts of rapid technological development on the environment shared by all. Chapter 1 described the gradual accommodation of the American economy to the presence of these programs in the past four decades; it is an exercise of ideological fantasy to expect that such programs will lapse or be substantially constrained. Indeed, as chapter 8 suggests, there are areas of the system, crucial to its future growth, that seem to be calling for still more public programs.

Some of the costliest intrusions, in terms of government outlay, go beyond practical considerations to ethical justifications—efforts to achieve a fair, just, or compassionate society—to avoid extremes in the distribution of economic and noneconomic goods. These interventions reflect what might be called social compacts. They include social security, in which the young contribute to the support of the elderly; medical care, in which the healthy help to support the sick; unemployment compensation, in which the employed help to support the unemployed; the progressive income tax (made much less progressive in the 1980s), in which the rich carry some of the burdens of the poor. The programs that carry the costs of these social compacts are very large, very expensive; in terms of burdens on the system, they far outweigh all other intrusions. They account for the fact that the transfer payments flowing through the federal government now represent far and away the largest component of total federal outlay and enormously enhance the cost of government. They also reduce the raw economic incentives to work and to save. But they carry a very nearly invincible mandate.

Public opinion does not tend to formulate the issue quite this way, but it is clear enough that health care, education, and early opportunity cannot be allocated entirely by ability to pay, or the population will gradually develop a bipolar distribution, with the educated, employed, and healthy concentrated at one end, and the poor, uneducated, and disadvantaged at the other end. Such a polarized population would seem, in the end, to be incompatible with general one-man one-vote democracy. Expectations that the costs of programs to spread such essential goods more evenly can be easily contained, let alone reduced, are simply not well founded. We had better plan on the existing level of social costs continuing into the future. But we can hope that they will be more effective, better organized, better administered—in other words, that we will make use of the bitter lessons of past failures.

What lies ahead in institutional change in this area most certainly does not resemble the immense growth of intervention in the years from the 1930s to the 1970s. In Europe, as well as in the United States, the growth of interventions that bordered on revolution in those years has clearly abated; the rate has subsided to a more deliberate, more manageable, and less inflationary pace. It is far more widely recognized today than it was fifteen years ago that much of any incremental interventions will find their effects dissipated by renewed inflation, particularly if their methodology is weak and their management inadequate. Moreover, the self-interest that is the source of energy in a basically free-market system is still a principal motivation to efficient activity; this useful, dependable, and candid, if not inspiring, motivation has achieved new respect throughout the developed world, and even in the developing world, as a consequence of the evidence pouring out of the formerly Communist countries of Eastern Europe. The mixed economy appears to have approached a condition of general maturity in the United States and in most other developed economies.

But the American economy of the 1990s, having experienced almost fifteen years of institutional stability and even some withdrawal, here and there, with respect to intervention, seems to be moving toward a new round of reexamination and a fresh start in attacking the tough and resistant problems described in chapter 8. It can be hoped that the new round will be focused much more intensely on the specific problems of education, job opportunity, medical care, and living conditions at the bottom of the income distribution. Such programs can be expensive, but they will not fundamentally alter the structure of the system as the enormous new responsibilities undertaken by government after the 1920s certainly did. The weak economic performance and remaining large inequities in the system described in chapter 8 are pressing government toward further action, and surveys reveal that the public-at-large will support such extended programs. It would be foolish not to expect a considerable government response to these issues, with perhaps considerable incremental costs to the system as a whole. We should, accordingly, expect nothing in the way of significant tax relief in the 1990s.

The mixed economy is not a beautiful structure; it defies and irritates theoretical purists of all persuasions. It will doubtless continue to do so in the 1990s. Complex, changing, nontheoretical, it is the real world in which we live, the world reflected in the diverse and often conflicting numbers that describe the oncoming future. It is a living, changing reality that has evolved as a continuing resolution of the pressures between a democratic political system and a market-oriented economy. The evolutionary process will doubtless continue into the 1990s, and will require continuous close observation if the endless stream of numbers on the system is to be interpreted intelligently.

Appendix A

Alphabetical List of Series

For additional information about series listed in this appendix, please contact the following agencies:

Commodity Research Bureau
Suite 1820
30 South Wacker Drive
Chicago, Illinois 60606
Telephone: (1-800) 621-5271

The Conference Board
845 Third Avenue
New York, New York 10022
Telephone: (212) 759-0900

Department of the Treasury
3021 GAO Building
Washington, D.C. 20226
Telephone: (202) 208-1709

Federal Reserve Board
Publications Systems, Mail Stop 138
Washington, D.C. 20551
Telephone: (202) 452-3244 or 3245

National Bureau of Economic
  Research
1050 Massachusetts Avenue
Cambridge, Massachusetts 02138
Telephone: (617) 868-3905

Office of Management and Budget
Old Executive Office Building, N.W.
Washington, D.C. 20503
Telephone: (202) 395-3000

Standard and Poor's Corporation,
  Inc.
25 Broadway
New York, New York 10004
Telephone: (212) 208-1199

University of Michigan
Surveys of Consumers
P. O. Box 1248
Ann Arbor, Michigan 48106
Telephone: (313) 763-5224

U.S. Department of Commerce
Bureau of Economic Analysis (BEA)
1401 "K" Street, N.W.
Washington, D.C. 20230
Telephone: (202) 377-2000

U.S. Department of Labor
441 "G" Street, N.W.
Washington, D.C. 20212
Telephone: (202) 523-6666

Appendix B:

Approximate Release Dates for Monthly Statistics *

MONDAY	TUESDAY	WEDNESDAY	THURSDAY	FRIDAY
1 • Construction Expenditures ▲ • NAPM Index • Interest Rates • Merchandise Trade	**2** • Leading Indicators • New Hone Sales	**3** • Manufacturers' Shipments, Inventories, Orders ▲ • Auto Sales • Help-Wanted Index ▲	**4** • Jobless Claims○	**5** • Employment • TCB Diffusion Index
8	**9** • Consumer Credit ▲	**10**	**11** • Jobless Claims ○ • Producer Prices • Retail Sales	**12** • Consumer Prices • Business Inventories ▲ • Real Earnings
15 • Housing Completions	**16** • Housing Starts and Permits • Industrial Production • Capacity Utilization	**17**	**18** • Jobless Claims ○	**19** • Michigan Consumer Confidence • Federal Deficit
22	**23**	**24** • Advance Durable Goods Orders	**25** • Jobless Claims • Existing Home Sales • Import and Export Prices	**26** • Personal Income and PCE
29 • New Home Sales • Farm Prices	**30** • Leading Indicators • TCB Consumer Confidence			

✳ For prior month, unless otherwise indicated
▲ For two months prior
○ For two weeks prior

Appendix C:

Approximate Release Dates for Quarterly Statistics ✳

MONDAY	TUESDAY	WEDNESDAY	THURSDAY	FRIDAY
1	**2** • U.S. International Transactions	**3**	**4** • Plant and Equipment Expenditures ▲	**5** • Collective Bargaining Settlements
8	**9** • Housing Vacancies	**10**	**11**	**12** • Flow of Funds ▲▲
15 • Quarterly Financial Report, Manufacturing	**16** • Current Account Balance	**17** • Productivity and Costs	**18**	**19**
22	**23**	**24**	**25** • Gross Domestic Product • Personal Income • Corporate Profits	**26**
29	**30**			

✳ For prior quarter, unless otherwise indicated
▲ For current quarter
▲▲ For two quarter prior

About the Authors

Albert T. Sommers is among the most widely respected economists serving the U.S. business community. In his more than forty years at The Conference Board, thirteen of them as its chief economist, he has advised literally hundreds of companies on economic conditions and the future course of the U.S. economy.

Mr. Sommers is currently senior fellow and economic counsellor to The Conference Board. He has been economic adviser to The Ford Foundation, The American Express Company, and Bankers Trust Company, among others. He is a director of several industrial and financial institutions and of the National Bureau of Economic Research, a Fellow of the National Association of Business Economists, and a former member of the Columbia University economics faculty. He is the editor and publisher of "The Sommers Letter," a continuing appraisal of the national and international economic outlook, read by more than 2,500 business executives and government officials, both here and abroad.

Lucie R. Blau, an economist and assistant to the senior fellow and economic counsellor at The Conference Board, has collaborated with Mr. Sommers on a host of publications, extending over three decades, and is an assistant editor of "The Sommers Letter." She holds advanced degrees in education and community relations research.

About The Conference Board

Founded in 1916, The Conference Board's twofold purpose is to improve the business enterprise system and to enhance the contribution of business to society.

To accomplish this, The Conference Board strives to be the leading global business membership organization that enables senior executives from all industries to explore and exchange ideas of impact on business policy and practices. To support this activity, The Conference Board provides a variety of forums and a professionally managed research program that identifies and reports objectively on key areas of changing management concern, opportunity, and action.

Nonprofit and nonpartisan, The Conference Board is supported by more than 2,500 companies, trade associations, government agencies, labor unions, colleges and universities, and individuals. The Board has offices in the United States, Europe, and Canada.